100 MANDELA MOMENTS

100 MANDELA MOMENTS

Kate Sidley

Jonathan Ball Publishers
Johannesburg & Cape Town

Published in South Africa in 2018 by
JONATHAN BALL PUBLISHERS
A division of Media24 (Pty) Ltd
PO Box 33977
Jeppestown
2043

ISBN 978-1-86842-902-8
ebook ISBN 978-1-86842-903-5

*Every effort has been made to trace the copyright holders and to obtain their
permission for the use of copyright material. The publishers apologise for any
errors or omissions and would be grateful to be notified of any corrections
that should be incorporated in future editions of this book.*

Twitter: www.twitter.com/JonathanBallPub
Facebook: www.facebook.com/JonathanBallPublishers
Blog: http://jonathanball.bookslive.co.za/

Cover photo: Nelson Mandela at a news conference ahead of the second
46664 concert near George, in the Western Cape, on 18 March 2005.
(Reuters/Mike Hutchings)

Cover by Michiel Botha
Design and typesetting by Nazli Jacobs
Set in ITC Stone Serif

solutions
Printed by **novus print**, a Novus Holdings company

CONTENTS

TIMELINE

1918   18 July: Nelson Mandela born at Mvezo, in the
Eastern Cape

1939   enrols at University College of Fort Hare

1941   comes to Johannesburg

1943   joins the African National Congress (ANC)

1944   marries Evelyn Mase; forms the ANC Youth League

1948   National Party comes to power

1952   Defiance Campaign begins; Mandela sets up law
practice with Oliver Tambo; arrested for violating the
Suppression of Communism Act and given suspended
sentence

1955   ANC adopts the Freedom Charter

1956   Mandela arrested and charged with treason; start of
Treason Trial

1958   divorces Evelyn and marries Winnie Madikizela

1960   Sharpeville massacre; State of Emergency declared;
ANC and PAC banned

1961   South Africa becomes a republic

1961   Mandela is acquitted of treason, goes underground

1961   Umkhonto we Sizwe (MK) is formed

1962   Mandela secretly leaves the country for military
training in Africa

1962	arrested and sentenced to five years' imprisonment for leaving the country illegally
1963	charged with sabotage in the Rivonia Trial
1964	begins life sentence on Robben Island
1982	transferred to Pollsmoor Prison
1985	State of Emergency declared
1986	second State of Emergency declared
1988	Mandela transferred to Victor Verster Prison
1990	ANC and other liberation organisations unbanned and Mandela freed after 27 years in prison
1993	Mandela awarded the Nobel Peace Prize (with FW de Klerk)
1994	first democratic election; Mandela inaugurated as President of South Africa on 10 May
1997	steps down as ANC president
1998	marries Graça Machel on his 80th birthday
1999	steps down as President of South Africa
2004	retires from public life
2013	5 December: Death of Nelson Mandela

MANDELA
THE BOY

NAMING RITES

On 18 July 1918 at Mvezo, a tiny village in the district of Umtata (today Mthatha), a baby was born to Nosekeni Fanny and Gadla Henry Mphakanyiswa. The baby's father was a chief and an advisor to the local king, and they were a family of some standing in the community, minor royalty of the Thembu tribe. This new baby would grow up in the royal household, although he was not in line to the throne.

The child was named Rolihlahla Mandela. The literal meaning of the isiXhosa name Rolihlahla is 'pulling the branch of a tree', but it is more generally understood to mean 'troublemaker'. There's an old saying that a loved child has many names, and this was the first of many names assigned to the child by family, culture and affection.

The day he started school, the teacher gave every child an English name, as was then the custom. His new name was Nelson, which he later speculated might have been for Lord Nelson, the great British naval hero.

In his long life, Nelson Rolihlahla Mandela both caused and experienced trouble, and proved himself to be a great leader. So perhaps the names were well chosen.

Madiba, his clan name, referred to the Thembu chief who

ruled the Transkei in the 18th century. In later years, Mandela was widely and affectionately known by this name.

Once he had been through the traditional Xhosa initiation ritual, Mandela was given the name Dalibhunga, which means 'founder of the council'.

His city friends sometimes called him Nel when he was a young man. Over time, Mandela became known, affectionately, as Tata, the isiXhosa for 'father'. And then Khulu, a shortened form of the word for 'grandfather'. Old struggle comrades sometimes referred to him as 'the old man'.

OF DONKEYS AND DISHONOUR

A young Nelson Mandela and the local boys were taking turns to jump up onto the back of an unruly donkey. When his turn came, just as Mandela jumped up, the beast bolted into the nearby thornbush and he was soon thrown, scratched and bloody, to the ground, much to his humiliation (and, doubtless, the great amusement of the other boys).

Mandela's autobiography, *Long Walk to Freedom*, describes how this childhood humiliation taught him a lesson. He wrote: 'I had lost face among my friends. Even though it was a donkey that unseated me, I learned that to humiliate another person is to make him suffer an unnecessarily cruel fate. Even as a boy, I defeated my opponents without dis-honouring them.'

It was just one of many lessons he learned growing up in the small village of Qunu. Mandela spent his time play-ing in the veld with the village boys, stick-fighting, gathering fruit and honey, catching birds and fish, walking the hills and swimming the streams, and tending and herding cattle. It was an upbringing that gave him a deep and long-lasting love of the land. Much later, during his years in prison, he would think back to those days and write about the simple pleasures of a rural childhood – drinking milk straight from a cow's udder, roasting mielies over an open fire.

Mandela was to face many powerful and oppressive oppo-nents. While he fought them courageously, with full force, when the time came that he had the power, he allowed them the opportunity to come over to his side without humiliation.

SCHOOL DAYS

At seven years of age, Rolihlahla was given a cut-down pair of his father's trousers, held up with a piece of string, and sent to school. It doesn't sound particularly remarkable, but he was the first person in his family to go to a formal school.

It was the word of a retired schoolteacher that set Nelson

Mandela on his educational path. This man, George Mbeka, was a friend of Mandela's father, and an exception in the village, being both educated and Christian. One day, he paid a visit to Rolihlahla's mother and said, 'Your son is a clever young fellow. He should go to school.'

She didn't know what to make of this completely unexpected suggestion – no one in the family had ever been to school, and neither she nor her husband was literate – but she did relay it to her husband, who decided that their youngest son would be the first.

And off he went, in his too-big trousers, to the one-room school over the hill from his home.

THE ROYAL HOUSE

Unexpectedly, Rolihlahla had to leave the village of Qunu, the only home he'd ever had, the huts and fields and pastures he'd played in and the children he'd known all his life. His father had died of tuberculosis and his mother announced that they were leaving Qunu.

Mother and son set out on foot. The place they came to was grand by comparison, a large whitewashed home with a fine garden, vegetables and flowers and fruit trees, and large healthy herds of cattle and sheep. Even a motorcar! This was the Great Place in Mqhekezweni, the royal residence of his father's cousin, Jongintaba Dalindyebo, the regent of the Thembu people. He was to become Mandela's guardian and benefactor. The regent's handsome son Justice was to become his older brother and best friend.

Without any display of sentiment, just a tender look, Mandela's mother left her boy in the place where he was to be raised and educated in a style that she could not provide. He was nine years old, and adapted eagerly to his new world.

At the local school, Mandela studied English, Xhosa, History and Geography, and again this clever boy caught the attention of his teachers (although he would attribute his success more to doggedness and self-discipline than to cleverness). But he learned as much from watching and listening to the chiefs and headmen who came to the Great Place to consult the regent and settle disputes. He heard tales of African heroes and warriors, the likes of which he'd never known. He heard of the evil white Queen across the waters. It was an important formative time. He internalised the notion of ubuntu – that we are bound to each other, as humans, in mutual compassion and respect.

He paid attention as cases were presented and adjudicated at tribal meetings, intrigued by his first taste of legal matters. Mandela later wrote that his own ideas of leadership were profoundly influenced by the regent and his court. Every man who came before the court was heard, from the grandest to the most modest, and the regent listened without interrupting. The meetings would continue until consensus was reached. Mandela regarded this as the purest democracy, and followed the principles himself in his political life. He would always remember Jongintaba's view that a leader should shepherd his flock using gentle persuasion, drawing strays back to join the main body of the flock.

BECOMING A MAN

It was time for young Rolihlahla to become a man. He was 16, but his age was not the defining factor. In Xhosa tradition, a boy becomes a man through initiation and circumcision. Without going through this ritual, no matter how old he is, he remains a boy. Traditionally, he may not marry, or inherit, or officiate in tribal rituals, without taking this important step.

A group of boys take this journey from boyhood to manhood together, isolated from the rest of society. Mandela was to go through the initiation ritual alongside Justice and other boyhood friends, 26 in all.

It was customary for the boys to perform some brave deed before the ceremony. In the old days, this might have been a battle or raid, but in his time any daring deed would do. They decided to steal a pig, luring it out of its kraal with a trail of the sediment from homemade beer. The old pig 'gradually made his way to us, wheezing and snorting, and eating the sediment. When he got near us, we captured the poor pig, slaughtered it, and then built a fire and ate roast pork under the stars. No piece of pork has ever tasted as good before or since.'

In his autobiography, Mandela describes this as a sacred time, enjoying the last days of his boyhood with his fellow initiates.

After circumcision – which must be endured in stoic silence, except for the cry of 'I am a man!' – he was given the name Dalibhunga, meaning 'Founder of the Bungha', the traditional ruling body of the Transkei.

Mandela recounts his reaction to the speech Chief Meligqili made at the great ceremony that ended the initiates' seclusion, in which he honoured the young men and the ritual they had been part of, and then changed tack, telling them that the promise of manhood is an illusion: 'For we Xhosas, and all black South Africans, are a conquered people. We are slaves in our own country. We are tenants on our own soil . . . The abilities, the intelligence, the promise of these young men will be squandered in their attempt to eke out a living doing the simplest, most mindless chores for the white man . . .'

Mandela was angry at the chief's 'ignorant' remarks spoiling his proud and special day. But, he wrote, 'His words began to work on me. He had sown a seed, and though I let that seed lie dormant for a long season, it eventually began to grow. Later I realised that the ignorant man that day was not the chief but myself.'

As well as marking his entry into manhood, initiation marked the first stirrings of political consciousness.

BROADENING HORIZONS

There was dancing and singing. A sheep was slaughtered. It was a great occasion. And it was all in honour of young Rolihlahla Nelson Mandela.

One day, this man would head political organisations. He would be awarded a Nobel Peace Prize. He would be inaugurated as President of South Africa. But this was the first celebration held in his honour and the achievement was relatively modest – he had finished and passed primary school, and was soon to make his way to high school. Mandela was delighted at the celebration, and at the regent's gift – the boy's first pair of boots.

The regent had plans for Mandela. And they did not include working in the white man's gold mines. He was to become a counsellor to the king, and that meant he needed an education. He enrolled at Clarkebury Boarding Institute, which was the oldest Wesleyan mission and the best school for Africans in the Transkei. It had particular significance to the Thembu royal family. Mandela's great-grandfather had been instrumental in the founding of the school, having given the land on which it was built. The regent himself had studied there, as had his son Justice.

Clarkebury was strict, rigorous and hierarchical – a real change from the village school. Here Mandela met African teachers with university degrees, and the Reverend Cecil Harris, the school governor, whom the regent considered a white Thembu.

Mandela soon discovered that no one was particularly impressed by his illustrious lineage – he was just one of the boys. And a country boy at that. Clomping around in his unfamiliar new boots, 'like a horse in spurs', he drew teasing and laughter from the girls, to his fury and humiliation.

He soon found his feet. He went on to pass the three-year programme in two years, and followed Justice to Healdtown, the Wesleyan college at Fort Beaufort. It was one of the biggest schools for Africans on the continent, with more than 1 000 pupils, and was strictly run on the English model, with a largely Eurocentric curriculum focused on British history, geography and culture.

Renowned Xhosa poet and praise singer Krune Mqhayi came to Healdtown, and his visit struck the young scholar 'like a comet streaking across the night sky'. The students and staff were assembled in the dining hall, at the end of which was a stage. A door led from the stage to the house of the principal, Dr Wellington. 'The door itself was nothing special,' Mandela wrote. 'But we thought of it as

Dr Wellington's door, for no one ever walked through it except Dr Wellington himself.'

The door opened and in came the poet, dramatically dressed in a traditional leopard-skin kaross and hat, carrying a spear in each hand. Mandela later wrote: 'The sight of a black man in tribal dress coming through that door was electrifying. It is hard to explain the impact it had on us. It seemed to turn the universe upside down . . . At one point, he raised his assegai into the air for emphasis, and accidentally hit the curtain wire above him, which made a sharp noise and caused the curtain to sway . . . He faced us, and newly energised, exclaimed that this incident – the assegai striking the wire – symbolised the clash between the culture of Africa and that of Europe. His voice rose and he said: ". . . the assegai stands for what is glorious and true in African history; it is a symbol of the African as warrior and the African as artist . . ."'

The poet railed against foreigners who did not care for African culture: 'One day, the forces of African society will achieve a momentous victory over the interloper. For too long we have succumbed to the false gods of the white man. But we shall emerge and cast off these foreign notions.' Mandela was astonished, galvanised and conflicted by this powerful, outspoken speaker, and never forgot him.

AMONG THE INTELLECTUAL ELITE

In 1939, Nelson Mandela enrolled at the University College of Fort Hare. The institution had been going for just two decades, and had only 200 students, but it was the home of the black intellectual elite, many of whom would go on to become leaders.

Mandela loved Fort Hare. He was exposed to new ideas, brilliant minds and all manner of pursuits, intellectual, physical and social. He joined the drama society and learned ballroom dancing. He played soccer and competed in cross-country running. He wrote that the latter sport taught him to compensate for his lack of natural running talent with diligence and discipline: 'I applied this to everything I did. Even as a student, I saw many young men who had great natural ability, but who did not have the self-discipline and patience to build on their endowment.'

It was here that Mandela first met Oliver Tambo, who would go on to become his law partner, comrade and be-loved lifelong friend. Tambo was a top scholar and debater and, unlike Mandela, was already politically active. The two were not close during their university days, and there was as yet no indication that their lives would be intimately entwined for decades to come.

Mandela's mentor at the time was Kaiser Matanzima, who, although he was Mandela's nephew, was older and more confident and sophisticated than Mandela, and destined to be a king of the Thembu line. At the time, Mandela idolised KD, as he was called, and the two were always to be found in each other's company. Tall and well turned out, they cut quite a dash. Matanzima remembered of them at that time: 'The two of us were very handsome young men, and all the women wanted us.'

Their close relationship would not last. Their political trajectories couldn't have been more different. While Mandela found his home in the African National Congress (ANC), Matanzima became 'state president' of the Transkei and a champion of the apartheid government's 'homeland' system, which created sham independent states to which black South Africans were assigned according to their ethnicity.

PRINCIPALS AND PRINCIPLES

It was while he was at Fort Hare that Mandela first clashed with authority over a matter of principle, showing the 'proud rebelliousness, stubborn sense of fairness' that he believed he had inherited from his father. He was two years into his studies when he was faced with a difficult decision that would have a significant impact on his life.

Ahead of the election of the Student Representative Council (SRC), students raised their grievances – poor food, and not enough real power to the SRC – and agreed to boycott the election unless the university authorities accepted their demands. Mandela was among the six representatives elected by the small minority of students who did vote. The representatives resigned. A second vote was held with the same result – a small turnout, and the same six representatives. This time, the other representatives agreed to stay on the SRC – but not Nelson Mandela. In the belief that this result did not represent the will of the majority of students, Mandela resigned his position.

The university principal, Dr Kerr, asked him to reconsider, and warned Mandela that if he insisted on resigning from the SRC, he would be expelled.

This left Mandela with a difficult decision to make – whether to follow the path that he felt certain was the morally correct one and sabotage his academic career, or to stand down and complete his degree.

He followed his principles and his own sense of agency, as he explains in his autobiography: 'I knew it was foolhardy for me to leave Fort Hare, but at the moment when I needed to compromise, I simply could not do so . . . I resented his absolute power over my fate. I should have had every right to resign from the SRC if I wished . . .'

ESCAPE TO THE CITY OF GOLD

When Mandela returned to Mqhekezweni after his exams, his guardian, the Thembu regent, Jongintaba Dalindyebo, was not at all pleased with what he regarded as the young man's inexplicable and nonsensical stand at Fort Hare. Why throw away a promising career over such a matter? He told Mandela to do as the principal wanted – apologise and return to university.

A few weeks into the break, the regent summoned his son Justice and Mandela, and dropped a bombshell – he had arranged marriages for them both to girls from good families. These were young women whom they knew but had no attraction or particular affection for – in fact, the girl chosen for Mandela had long been in love with Justice. No matter, lobola was arranged, and the marriages were to take place immediately.

This was all within the provisions of Thembu law, and it was not for the two young men to argue. Again, Mandela was in a bind. The regent had taken him in after the death of his father, brought him up as his own son, and paid for his education. Mandela owed him a great deal. But an unwanted marriage to a young woman he did not love? No. Mandela, the self-described romantic, was not going to have

someone else choose a bride for him – even if that someone was the regent. Justice felt the same. In defiance of
tradition and authority, they decided to reject the regent's
plan. In that time and place, this was a deeply rebellious act.
The two young men hatched a plan to run away to Johannesburg. To fund their escape, they sold two of the regent's
prize oxen to a local trader.

And so, in 1941, began Mandela's life in the fabled city
of gold, glittering with electric light and possibility. Here,
after a brief stint as a watchman on the mines, he made a
start on the things that would define him – his law career,
love and family, and his developing political consciousness.

He had left Fort Hare without completing his degree, but
Mandela had not given up on his ambition to become a
lawyer. A helpful cousin offered to introduce him to an
influential businessman and local leader who worked in
the property business and might be able to help. That man
was Walter Sisulu.

Sisulu listened to Mandela's story – the trouble at Fort
Hare, his determination to become a lawyer, his intention
to study by correspondence. He described their first meeting in an interview: 'I was at once struck by the personality
of Nelson. I had, by the way, at this time already joined the
African National Congress and was able to attend the
conferences of the ANC. And so when he came I found a
person who just answered my hope, my aspiration. This is
a young man who must be developed, who has a great part

to play in the movement. His personality was very striking, very warm. If he had not come the next day, I would have gone looking for him.'

Sisulu, with his fine intellect, was to become a mentor to Mandela. Many years later, in 2011, Mandela, speaking at Sisulu's funeral, said: 'From the moment when we first met he has been my friend, my brother, my keeper, my comrade.' Sisulu's more immediate influence was to introduce Mandela to Lazar Sidelsky, a progressive white lawyer. And so Mandela got his first job in a law firm, working as a clerk while he completed his degree.

Mandela was poor, sometimes travelling on foot the 20 kilometres from his home in Alexandra township to his job in town, to save the bus fare. But he was making a start on his career, supporting himself and expanding his horizons in the big city, Johannesburg. It was here that he made his first white friend, was invited to multiracial get-togethers, first came across communists, earned his BA degree. Here, he fell in love and had children. He started a law firm. And it was here that he developed the political ideas and consciousness that would come to define his life.

MANDELA
THE
YOUNG
MAN

FOUNDING THE ANC YOUTH LEAGUE

The Sisulu house in Orlando was a home-from-home for Nelson Mandela and other activists. The welcoming atmosphere, enthralling political discussion and Ma Sisulu's cooking drew them, and it was here that Mandela met someone who would have a lasting influence on his life – Anton Lembede.

One of the few African lawyers of the time, Lembede was possessed of multiple degrees, a brilliant and unusual mind, and a magnetic personality. His views on African nationalism struck a chord with Mandela, Tambo, Sisulu, Peter Mda, Dr Lionel Majonbozi and others. To these young men, the ANC leadership seemed old, tired and insufficiently militant. A Youth League would be just the thing to shake – and wake – things up, and to press the ANC into mass action.

Mandela was part of a delegation, led by Lembede, to propose the idea to Dr Alfred Xuma, the president of the ANC. Xuma felt that the ANC wasn't ready for mass action, but they continued to work on a manifesto for the new body. And so, on Easter Sunday 1944, the ANC Youth League (ANCYL) was formed at the Bantu Men's Social Centre in Eloff Street. It was made up of a small group – 100 or so – of mostly Fort Hare students, trade unionists and other smart young men with a passionate belief in African nationalism. They were wary of communists and the white left. They believed Africans would be freed only by their own efforts, and regarded themselves as the 'brains-trust and power-house' of African nationalism.

Lembede was elected the Youth League's first president, and Oliver Tambo its first secretary. Mandela was on the executive committee, as was Sisulu. Hard as it is to imagine, Mandela admitted to being intimidated by the political astuteness and eloquence of his fellow Youth Leaguers.

Sadly, Lembede died suddenly in July 1947, at the age of 33. At a meeting to discuss ANCYL business, he complained to Mandela of chills and a sudden stomach pain. His colleagues drove him to hospital, but he died that night. It was a great loss to the movement.

FIRST LOVE

It wasn't just Lembede whom Mandela met at the busy Sisulu house. It was there that he met Walter's cousin Evelyn Mase, who was to become his first wife. 'She was a quiet, pretty girl, who did not seem overawed by the comings and goings,' he wrote. Evelyn was from the Transkei, like her soon-to-be husband, and was staying at the Sisulus' house while training as a nurse at the Johannesburg non-European General Hospital.

Evelyn and Nelson fell in love and were married at the Native Commissioner's Court on 5 October 1944, with Walter and Albertina Sisulu as witnesses.

In 1946, they moved into a two-room municipal house in Orlando East, and their first son, Madiba Thembekile (Thembi), was born. Mandela has written about how he enjoyed the domesticity – entertaining guests in his own home, bathing his baby boy – but had little time for it, given his other commitments. Politics took up much of his time, and in 1947 he gave up his job to study for his Bachelor of Law degree. Evelyn supported the family on her salary.

A second child, a baby girl, was born, but Makaziwe was sickly and frail and died at nine months – a devastating loss. A boy, Makgatho, followed, and then another daughter, also named Makaziwe in honour of the first daughter they had lost.

The marriage was under strain from many quarters. In 1953, Evelyn spent months away from home on a midwifery course in Durban while relatives moved into the house to take care of the young children. Mandela's schedule was relentless, between his increasing political involvement and the law office he opened with Oliver Tambo. Evelyn wanted him to give up politics and take the family back to the Transkei.

The difference in their worldviews was exacerbated when Evelyn became a Jehovah's Witness. Her devotion to her religion matched Mandela's devotion to the struggle. The conflict between their beliefs became untenable and began to engulf their children. While Mandela talked politics to the children, Evelyn took them to church and to distribute *The Watchtower* magazine. Their differences were irreconcilable.

Matters came to a head when Mandela was arrested for treason. He returned home on bail to find his house empty – even the curtains had been removed – and his wife and children gone. In 1957, thirteen years after they married, the couple divorced.

The break-up was hard on the children, and their hurt pained Mandela deeply. Mandela wrote in his autobiography: 'She was a very good woman, charming, strong and faithful, and a good mother. I never lost my respect and admiration for her, but in the end, we could not make our marriage work.'

Thereafter, Evelyn returned to the Eastern Cape and opened a grocery store, which supported her and her children. In 1998, she married Soweto businessman Simon Rakeepile, also a Jehovah's Witness.

'WHEN I MET MANDELA . . .'

It's not often that we recall a first meeting with a dear friend, but advocate George Bizos remembers the first time he spoke to the man who was to become his client (repeatedly!) and his lifelong friend. It was in 1948, after a mass student meeting in the Great Hall at Wits University that had been called in response to government plans to introduce a racially based quota system. Bizos, a 21-year-old first-year BA student, stood up and made an impromptu speech, with the proposal that they give the government an ultimatum: if the quota was implemented, the students would strike.

Bizos made it onto the front page of the Afrikaans daily newspaper *Die Transvaler*, which was suitably scandalised by his statement: 'If advocating equal treatment for my fellow students makes me a leftist then I am proud to be one!'

'And so it was,' Bizos recalled in his memoir, *65 Years of Friendship*, 'that a few days later, Nelson Mandela strode up to me on the steps of the Great Hall, smiling his wonderful smile. He did not have to introduce himself, although, of course, he did. Like most students on campus I knew who he was. I had heard him speak.'

At this time, Mandela was 30 years old and in what should have been the final year of his Bachelor of Law degree. He was already a well-known political leader, and secretary-general of the ANC Youth League.

From the beginning, he made an impression on Bizos. For a start, Mandela cut a striking figure, with his height and his double-breasted suits and his shoes polished to a high gleam. 'He seemed to me to be a man of destiny, someone who knew that he had a role to play, but he was no egotist.

33

I noticed he hardly ever said "I" when discussing political matters – it was always "we" or "my organisation" or "the liberation movement".'

Back to that first conversation on the steps of the Great Hall. Mandela thanked Bizos for his public stand and told him that it meant a lot. Instead of moving on, he engaged the younger man on his background, and what had led him to make such a statement. Bizos launched into his history as a refugee from Nazi-occupied Greece. 'Nelson was already possessed of that genuine interest in other people that so defined him,' wrote Bizos. 'In this, our first proper conversation, I did all the talking. The generosity of Nelson's interest, the sheer charisma of his concentration, rendered me utterly at ease.'

Many friendships of great significance were forged at Wits, friendships that would influence the course of people's lives. Ismail Meer, JN Singh, Joe Slovo, Ruth First, Harold Wolpe, Bram Fischer, Arthur Chaskalson and Duma Nokwe are some of the remarkable leaders who came through the university at that time.

The friendship between Mandela and Bizos was to continue for 65 years. Even after Mandela's death, his friend and lawyer has continued to take care of his interests, acting as executor of his estate.

DEFIANCE CAMPAIGN VOLUNTEER-IN-CHIEF

On 6 April 1652 Jan van Riebeeck arrived at the Cape. The tercentenary of this day was celebrated by white South Africans in 1952, but black South Africans had nothing to celebrate. Since the National Party's election victory in 1948, racist laws were becoming increasingly onerous. The movement of black people was heavily controlled. Black men had to carry passes at all times and could stay only in designated areas, and the government planned to extend this requirement to black women.

Against this heightened repression, the Defiance Campaign was planned jointly by the ANC and the South African Indian Congress (SAIC) as a mass, non-violent passive resistance campaign. The idea was simple – for volunteers to peacefully defy the unjust, racist apartheid laws. Nelson Mandela, then president of the ANC Youth League, was appointed volunteer-in-chief, and was responsible for organising the campaign, raising funds and canvassing for volunteers. In the atmosphere of the time, he knew it was highly likely that a campaign of passive resistance would be met with the full force of the state. Putting himself at the forefront of breaking these unjust laws was a very courageous stance.

In the run-up to the campaign, Mandela was the main speaker at a rally of over 10 000 people in Durban. It was the biggest gathering he had ever addressed and he found it exhilarating. He emphasised the new unity between Africans, coloureds and Indians, and told them that with this campaign they would be making history.

On 26 June, the campaign went into gear. Groups of volunteers went into action, contravening pass laws and curfews, ignoring orders for the segregation of facilities, courting arrest. Their supporters accompanied them with freedom songs, cheers and cries of 'Afrika!' and 'Mayibuye!'

Leaving a meeting late one evening early in the campaign, Mandela and Yusuf Cachalia were approached by a policeman. 'Into the van,' he ordered. Mandela wrote: 'I felt like explaining to him that I was in charge of running the campaign on a day-to-day basis and was not scheduled to defy and be arrested until much later, but of course that would have been ridiculous. I watched as he arrested Yusuf, who burst out laughing at the irony of it all. It was a lovely sight to see him smiling as he was led away by police.'

Mandela and other leaders spent two days in prison – Mandela's longest incarceration to date – and were released.

But not for long. On 30 July, the police arrived at his place of work with a warrant. He was charged under the Suppression of Communism Act. Around the country, other leaders were arrested simultaneously. Twenty-one leaders appeared in court, including Ahmed Kathrada, Walter Sisulu, JB Marks,

Dr Yusuf Dadoo, Yusuf Cachalia and ANC president Dr James Moroka.

Their court appearances drew exuberant crowds to the Johannesburg Magistrate's Court. There was something new in this mass mobilisation of support – schoolchildren and university students and battle-scarred campaigners, people of all races and creeds joined together to support their leaders.

On 2 December 1952, the accused were found guilty and sentenced to nine months' imprisonment with hard labour, suspended for two years.

The campaign spread. By mid-December over 8 000 people had been arrested. The offences were minor, rarely attracting more than a few days in prison or a £10 fine. But the publicity was massive, and new members joined the ANC in droves.

Mandela said later that they were amateurs at this business of mass mobilisation, and made mistakes, but that the Defiance Campaign was significant in many ways. The ANC was finally established as a truly mass-based organisation. And Mandela himself had come of age as a freedom fighter.

MANDELA AND TAMBO ATTORNEYS

'Mandela and Tambo Attorneys', read the brass plate on the door of Chancellor House, a less-than-smart building in

Fox Street, Ferreirasdorp, the oldest part of Johannesburg. This was the law office of Nelson Mandela and Oliver Tambo. It was 1952, and this was one of the first black-owned and -operated law firms in the country. It was housed in one of the few buildings where African tenants could have offices, thanks to the Indian owner.

Because of the many restrictive and humiliating apartheid laws at the time, it was an easy matter for a black person to find themselves in need of legal help. The ways in which a black person might break the law were manifold: using a Whites Only bus or bench or beach, being on the street after 11 pm, not having a pass book or having a pass book but not having the right signature in it . . . The list went on and on.

A thousand black people a day were arrested for pass law violations. Black people were desperate for legal help and advice, and there was very little available. The new firm quickly stepped into that space. Tambo described the long queues that would greet them daily as they arrived at work, each person with a tale of injustice, suffering and humiliation.

Mandela didn't just provide legal advice; he inspired and fascinated. George Bizos recalled: 'Mandela did not act as though he were a black man in a white man's court, but rather as if everyone else was a guest in his. He cut a dashing figure, this imposing black man striding through the Whites Only entrance in his fine clothes. He was often featured in the press, and by the mid 1950s, he was a lawyer of some renown, the most well-known black lawyer in

Joburg.' Tambo didn't quite have Mandela's dramatic flair, but he was clever, highly moral, thoughtful and wise.

Dikgang Moseneke, who went on to become a Pan Africanist Congress (PAC) activist, a Robben Islander, an advocate and eventually Deputy Chief Justice of South Africa, recalled in his memoir, *My Own Liberator*: 'I was only nine years old when I saw this plaque but it left an indelible impression on me. I had accompanied my father into the city, where he had come to consult Mr Mandela over a compensation claim for his family's forced removal... I remained in the rather congested but quiet waiting room as my father was called into an office. That fleeting visit must have left something in me...'

Historian Luli Callinicos interviewed South African Communist Party (SACP) leader Chris Hani two weeks before his assassination in 1993. Hani said: 'We admired [Mandela and Tambo] because we saw in them a different type of intelligentsia; an intelligentsia which is selfless, which was not just concerned about making money, creating a comfortable situation for themselves, but an intelligentsia which had lots of time for the struggle of the oppressed people of South Africa.'

There was plenty of work but there were also plenty of challenges. They had only really got going when Mandela was charged under the Suppression of Communism Act for his role in the Defiance Campaign.

Both men were arrested in 1956 and tried for treason.

Charges against Tambo were dropped and he was released. He went into exile in 1960. The Treason Trial ran for four years and the defendants were acquitted in 1961.

During this time, the law firm in Chancellor House closed, but there were still many black South Africans in need of Mandela's legal help. In 1960, he moved his rooms to Ahmed Kathrada's apartment at 13 Kholvad House, close by.

'Although my practice had dissolved, my reputation as a lawyer was undimmed,' wrote Mandela in his autobiography, *Long Walk to Freedom*. 'Soon, the lounge of No 13 and the passage outside were crammed with clients. Kathy would return home and discover that the only room in which he could be alone was his kitchen.'

LOVE AND MARRIAGE

One of the defining moments of Nelson Mandela's life was when he first set eyes on Nomzamo Winifred (Winnie) Madikizela. He spotted the young woman by the side of the road, waiting for a bus, and was struck by her beauty. As luck – or fate? – would have it, a few weeks later he went into Oliver Tambo's office and who should be there but the beauty from the bus stop. He was delighted.

He wrote in his autobiography that, from their first meeting, he felt her spirit, courage and wilfulness immediately and was deeply stirred by her presence. He knew then and there that he wanted her as his wife.

He was 39, separated from his wife, Evelyn, the father of three young children, and charged in the Treason Trial. She was 22, and the first black female social worker at Baragwanath Hospital. Winnie was strong-willed, clever and glamorous, with a great eye for clothes and shoes. She wasn't politicised at this time.

He had a rival for her affections – none other than his nephew and friend Kaiser Matanzima – but Mandela prevailed. On 14 June 1958, Nelson and Winnie were married at her family home in Bizana, in Pondoland, in a large traditional ceremony. The groom had to get special permission to leave Johannesburg for his own wedding. The wedding was attended by as many of the ANC executive as were able to come, under the terms of their banning orders, as well as some uninvited guests in the form of security police.

It was not an easy time for the newlyweds. The Mandela and Tambo law firm was in trouble, with its two principals tied up as defendants in the Treason Trial. Mandela was fully occupied with the trial, the law practice and his political activities. Winnie's modest salary supported the household, which soon included two daughters, Zindizwa (Zindzi) and Zenani.

Despite the pressures on the family, Mandela's friends attest that the couple was happy and in love. He was proud of Winnie, who became increasingly politicised and joined

41

the ANC Women's League, and was one of thousands of women arrested during protests at the central pass office.

They were married for more than three decades, but for most of that time they were apart. Nelson Mandela would soon be in exile, and then in prison. Winnie was permitted to visit her husband on Robben Island only once or twice a year, and their relationship was conducted through letters. She was subjected to constant police harassment, solitary confinement, banning and then banishment to the remote town of Brandfort in the Free State. To Nelson Mandela's great sadness, upon his release their marriage was strained from the outset, and he was left lonely. In 1996, they divorced, citing irreconcilable differences as the reason.

IN THE RING AND ON THE ROAD

There's an iconic picture of Nelson Mandela sparring on a Johannesburg rooftop with boxer Jerry Moloi. His stance is broad and stable, his fists are raised, and the right one is bandaged. On his face is a look of intense concentration; you can almost imagine him considering where to land his next punch. The photograph was taken by Bob Gosani and first appeared in *Drum* magazine, and something about it – the great leader as boxer – captured the public imagination. When Mandela was imprisoned, and pictures of him were unavailable, this particular image was widely admired and circulated.

Mandela claimed that, as a heavyweight, he had 'neither enough power to compensate for my lack of speed nor enough speed to make up for my lack of power'. Perhaps he was being overly modest. Who knows? But, whatever his prowess, he made boxing part of his life for decades.

He had boxed a bit at Fort Hare, but it was in Johannesburg that he started to take the sport more seriously, training daily for 90 minutes, often running the length of Commissioner Street. His son Thembi often accompanied him to the boxing club, and their shared training sessions were a rare and precious opportunity for father and son to be together.

The strenuous workout was a great stress reliever, and let him focus for a while on something other than the struggle and the law. He was intrigued by the strategy and science of boxing, and by how, even in apartheid South Africa, it was egalitarian. 'In the ring, rank, age, colour and wealth are irrelevant,' he wrote in *Long Walk to Freedom*.

His interest in the philosophy and strategy of boxing seems to have special significance when you consider his life as a fighter, leader, prisoner and negotiator: 'I was intrigued by how one moved one's body to protect oneself, how one used a strategy both to attack and retreat, how one paced oneself over a match.'

Outside the Jeppe Magistrate's Court in Market Street in

downtown Johannesburg, and across from the building that once housed the offices of Mandela and Tambo, you can see Marco Cianfanelli's sculpture *Shadow Boxing*, inspired by Gosani's famous photograph. At six metres high, the multi-faceted, painted mild-steel sculpture of Madiba is striking and instantly recognisable, and a popular stop-off and selfie point for tourists.

❦

THE PEOPLE SHALL GOVERN!

On a winter's day in a dusty field in the coloured township of Kliptown, south of Johannesburg, a remarkable convention was taking place. Most unusually for South Africa in 1955, the 3 000 people gathered here were of all races, creeds and colours. They were from all walks of life – workers, students, intellectuals, activists . . . And they were from all the anti-apartheid movements of the time: the African National Congress, the South African Indian Congress, the South African Coloured People's Congress, the Congress of Democrats (COD) and the South African Congress of Trade Unions (SACTU). Together, they made up the Congress Alliance.

Nelson Mandela watched quietly from a distance. He made no speeches. In fact, he went unnoticed by most of the delegates. He was in disguise, and his presence at this historic event was in defiance of his banning restrictions. He and other key activists and leaders – Walter Sisulu, Yusuf Cachalia, Yusuf Dadoo, Rusty and Hilda Bernstein – observed from a nearby yard.

This Congress of the People was perhaps the most representative gathering in the history of the country, and its task was to consider and then adopt a unique and powerful new document – the Freedom Charter, a vision for a united, non-racial and democratic South Africa.

How this document came to be is a fascinating story of democracy and consultation in action. In the early 1950s, the idea of a charter for South Africa, something similar to the Universal Declaration of Human Rights, was mooted. The idea was taken forward by the Congress Alliance, which brought together delegates from the main anti-apartheid bodies. All South Africans were invited to come forward with their demands for the kind of South Africa they wished to live in, so that these might be incorporated in a common document. A pamphlet titled *Let Us Speak of Freedom* was widely distributed. Thousands participated, sending in their ideas, hopes and dreams. These were collated and compiled into a single document – the Freedom Charter.

On the second day of the Congress of the People at Kliptown, the Freedom Charter was adopted.

It begins with these words:

We, the People of South Africa, declare for all our country and the world to know: that South Africa belongs to all who live in it, black and white, and that no government can justly claim authority unless it is based on the will of all the people; that our people have been robbed of their birthright to land, liberty and peace by a form of government founded on injustice and inequality; that our country will never be prosperous or free until all our people live in brotherhood, enjoying equal rights and opportunities; that only a democratic state, based on the will of all the people, can secure to all their birthright without distinction of colour, race, sex or belief; And therefore, we, the people of South Africa, black and white together – equals, countrymen and brothers – adopt this Freedom Charter. And we pledge ourselves to strive together, sparing neither strength nor courage, until the democratic changes here set out have been won.

The document goes on to outline these sacred rights – to land, to education, and so on – before concluding:

Let all who love their people and their country now say, as we say here:

'THESE FREEDOMS WE WILL FIGHT FOR, SIDE BY SIDE, THROUGHOUT OUR LIVES, UNTIL WE HAVE WON OUR LIBERTY.'

The Congress was brought to an abrupt close by police on the second day. But the document reverberated through the decades, in ways that could hardly have been imagined at the time. The government soon declared the Freedom Charter a communist document, and charged those involved – 156, including Nelson Mandela – with treason.

The Freedom Charter was to become the statement of the core principles of the member organisations of the Congress Alliance, and of all progressive people of South Africa. Four decades later, it would influence the new Constitution of the democratic South Africa.

THE POLICEMAN'S
KNOCK ON THE DOOR . . .

A sharp knock on the front door woke Nelson Mandela at 1.30 am on 5 December 1956. He knew immediately that this was the knock of the security police, and he was not wrong. There stood three policemen, who handed him a warrant for his arrest. The charge? High treason. They searched his house and his office, and delivered him to Johannesburg Prison, known as The Fort.

He later learned that all around the country, in the early hours of that morning, key members of the Congress Alliance were waking to those knocks. The swoop was executed with precision, and those arrested were flown in military aircraft to Johannesburg. The state planned to destroy the Congress Alliance once and for all.

One hundred and fifty-six people were charged with treason, which in those days carried the death penalty. The charges were based on the accused leaders' participation in drawing up the Freedom Charter, which, it was alleged, was a revolutionary communist document that would involve the violent overthrow of the state.

Outside the Drill Hall in Johannesburg, where the trial was to take place, protesters carried signs reading 'We Stand By Our Leaders'.

The list of defendants included much of the leadership of the democratic movement – Mandela, of course, as well as Chief Albert Luthuli, Oliver Tambo, Ahmed Kathrada, Ruth First, Helen Joseph and Joe Slovo. The mass arrests had the unintended consequence of bringing together the Congress Alliance leaders, including almost the entire executive committee of the ANC, as well as the SACP, the SAIC and the COD. Their consultation in the communal cells resulted in what Mandela described as 'the largest and longest unbanned meeting of the Congress Alliance in years'.

The case was remanded against most of the accused, and, in the end, 30 of them were in court for four years. The long trial, the time in prison and the endless dreary hours and days in the courtroom took a terrible toll on the defendants' lives and families. But, ironically, the ordeal strengthened the relationships between members of the Congress Alliance. As Rusty Bernstein wrote: 'Inter-racial trust and co-operation is a difficult plant to cultivate in the poisoned soil outside. It is somewhat easier in here where . . . the leaders of all ethnic factions of the movement are together and explore each other's doubts and reservations, and speak about them without constraint.'

Chief Albert Luthuli wrote in his foreword to Helen Joseph's book, *If This Be Treason*: 'The trial has been an inestimable blessing because it forged together diverse men and women of goodwill of all races who rallied to the support of the Treason Trial Fund and to keeping up the morale of the accused.' The fund was one of the first examples of foreign intervention in support of the anti-apartheid movement.

On 29 March 1961, the trial finally came to an end. The three-judge panel had reached a verdict: the state had failed to prove the ANC or the Freedom Charter as communist. After more than four years in court, the remaining accused were all acquitted of the charge of treason. The spectators cheered at the outcome, the crowd outside chanted and sang, the accused embraced their loved ones and laughed and cried. The party at Joe Slovo and Ruth First's house – a bois-terous, multiracial gathering that included the accused and lawyers, friends and family, as well as the usual uninvited guests in the form of security police – went on well into the night.

Mandela wrote that although the verdict was the right

one, it was a reflection only of the fairness of the individuals involved, not of the fairness of the system. In the wake of their humiliation at the Treason Trial, the government increasingly used tactics such as isolation and torture, and were less eager to observe prisoners' rights: 'The lesson they took away was not that we had legitimate grievances, but that they needed to be far more ruthless.'

The trial also spelled the end of Nelson Mandela's freedom. Soon after his acquittal, he would go underground.

MANDELA ON THE RUN

THE BLACK PIMPERNEL

With his arrest imminent, the ANC decided it was time for Nelson Mandela to go underground. On 26 June 1961, Mandela released a letter to South African newspapers:

I am informed that a warrant for my arrest has been issued, and that the police are looking for me. The National Action Council has given full and serious consideration to this question . . . and they have advised me not to surrender myself. I have accepted this advice, and will not give myself up to a Government I do not recognise . . .

I have chosen this course which is more difficult and which entails more risk and hardship than sitting in gaol. I have had to separate myself from my dear wife and children, from my mother and sisters to live as an outlaw in my own land. I have had to close my business, to abandon my profession, and live in poverty, as many of my people are doing . . .

I shall fight the Government side by side with you, inch by inch, and mile by mile, until victory is won. What are you going to do? Will you come along with us, or are you going to co-operate with the Government in its efforts to suppress the claims and aspirations of your own people? Are you going to remain silent and neutral in a matter of life and death to my people, to our people? For my own part I have made my choice. I will not leave South Africa, nor will I surrender. Only through hardship, sacrifice and militant action can freedom be won. The struggle is my life. I will continue fighting for freedom until the end of my days.

Nelson Mandela's life changed dramatically and irrevocably with that decision to go underground. He became the most wanted man in South Africa. He had no home to go to, moving from place to place, safe house to safe house, with only occasional visits from his family. He was on the run, in constant danger of discovery and arrest.

And it was an immense psychological shift. This proud and prominent leader, a lawyer, an imposing man of over six foot, had to make himself invisible and anonymous. The normally dapper Mandela cultivated an unkempt look and a scraggly beard. He wore blue workers' overalls, and posed as a 'garden boy' or a chauffeur. He would travel under the pretext of driving his 'master's' car.

The man on the run caught the imagination of the press, who dubbed him the Black Pimpernel – a reference to Emma Orczy's fictional Scarlet Pimpernel who evaded capture during the French Revolution, and about whom was written the famous lines: 'They seek him here, they seek him there. Those Frenchies seek him everywhere. Is he in heaven or is he in hell? That damned elusive Pimpernel.'

And damned elusive he was – a day here, a night there,

in empty flats, evading roadblocks. Ahmed Kathrada, who was tasked with organising Mandela's underground life, wrote that 'the police were hunting him relentlessly, and it was almost a full-time job keeping him out of their clutches. Rumours abounded – he's been spotted here, or there, he's escaped . . . He played up the myth of the Black Pimpernel, phoning newspaper reporters with stories of what we were planning or of the ineptitude of the police.'

'I would pop up here and there to the annoyance of the police and to the delight of the people,' wrote Mandela in *Long Walk to Freedom*.

One of the interviews he gave was with Patrick O'Donovan of *The Observer*, who observed drily: 'It seemed odd that he should not have been caught, but the tyranny was at that time mitigated by inefficiency and coarse stupidity.'

IN HIDING AND ON THE RUN

While he was on the run, Mandela's cover was almost blown on one occasion – by a bottle of milk!

He was living with SACP activist Wolfie Kodesh at the time, in a flat in a white area. Sour milk, or *amasi*, is a popular drink among black South Africans, and Mandela put a bottle of milk on the windowsill to go sour. One day he overheard three black guys outside the flat, discussing the milk: how is it that in this white area there is this bottle of milk outside, to make *amasi*? Who put it there? Surely not a white person?

Mandela and Kodesh were worried that this was the sort of mistake that could draw unwanted attention and even lead to Mandela's discovery. It was time to move on.

NO TO THE WHITE REPUBLIC

From underground, Mandela organised one last campaign of non-violent resistance, a stay-at-home campaign to protest the whites-only referendum that was held to decide whether South Africa should break ties with Britain and declare itself a republic. Needless to say, black South Africans were not entitled to vote. White voters were in favour, and on 31 May 1961 South Africa was declared a republic.

On 25 March, the ANC held an All-In African Conference in response to the referendum, and passed a resolution declaring that without the participation of the African people, no constitution had validity. The conference called for a non-racial national convention to prepare a democratic constitution.

Mandela proposed a three-day general strike, a mass stay-at-home campaign against what he called 'the unwanted republic'. The date was set for 29 May. In response to the call for the strike, Prime Minister HF Verwoerd mobilised the full might of the apartheid state. All police leave was cancelled and 5000 Citizen Force reservists were called up for duty. Meetings were banned, printing presses seized. Hundreds of activists were arrested, and new legislation was fast-tracked allowing police to detain prisoners for 12 days without bail. Armoured cars rumbled through the townships and helicopters fitted with powerful searchlights flew overhead. It was a massive and threatening show of force.

Much to Mandela's shock, the PAC undermined the strike, denouncing the ANC and telling people to ignore the call for a stay-at-home. The English-language press, which had been supportive, crumbled at the last minute and urged people to go to work.

On the first day of the strike, hundreds of thousands of people heeded the call to stay at home. Initially, it seemed a success – half of Johannesburg workers stayed at home – but as news filtered in from around the country, it became clear that the response was not enough. Mandela was disheartened and angry. For him, this was the final push for a non-violent, mass-based campaign against the state.

He told the press at the time: 'If the government reaction is to crush by naked force our non-violent struggle, we will have to reconsider our tactics. In my mind we are closing a chapter on this question of a non-violent policy.'

THE SPEAR OF THE NATION

The date 16 December is of great historical significance in South Africa. On this day in 1838, the Voortrekkers defeated the Zulu army at the Battle of Blood River. The Afrikaners commemorated this victory as the Day of the Vow, or Dingane's Day, and celebrated it as a public holiday.

On that same day in 1961, another significant historical event took place – the formation of the ANC's military wing, Umkhonto we Sizwe, the Spear of the Nation, known as MK.

The day marked a new role for Nelson Mandela. He was now a founder – and leader – of an armed force. 'I, who had never been a soldier, who had never fought in battle, who had never fired a gun at an enemy, had been given the task of starting an army. It would be a daunting task for a veteran general much less a military novice.'

The decision to embark on an armed struggle had not been an easy one, nor did it have unanimous support. Mandela had a lot of convincing to do.

For some – including Chief Albert Luthuli – non-violence was a core principle of the ANC, not some tactic that could be abandoned. Mandela believed the opposite – that it was a tactic that no longer worked.

Yusuf Cachalia, Dr Monty Naicker and JN Singh were

among those who opposed the armed struggle. Amina Cachalia related in her memoir: 'While Yusuf came to accept that the armed struggle was part of the liberation movement, it was against his Gandhian principles of non-violence, and he was never willing (nor was he ever asked) to be part of the armed struggle.'

There were others, such as Moses Kotane, who argued that engaging the powerful apartheid state militarily would bring down more violence and repression.

But Mandela convinced the naysayers that there was no choice. He employed an old African expression: 'The attacks of the wild beast cannot be averted with only bare hands.' Violence was inevitable, the state had seen to that. You just had to look at the Sharpeville shootings on 21 March 1960, when police opened fire on a crowd of protesters demonstrating against the pass laws, killing 69 people.

There was a political reality, too. There was a growing frustration with non-violence, both among the people and in organisations. A move to armed struggle was in the air. The Communist Party, the PAC and others were already moving in that direction. The ANC risked being out of step and out of control.

Mandela immediately recruited Joe Slovo, Walter Sisulu, Jack Hodgson and Rusty Bernstein. Homemade bombs exploded in power stations and government offices in Johannesburg, Port Elizabeth and Durban, and leaflets were circulated announcing the formation and the manifesto of MK:

The time comes in the life of any nation when there remain only two choices – submit or fight. That time has now come to South Africa. We shall not submit and we have no choice but to hit back by all means in our power in defence of our people, our future, and our freedom . . .

In a neat turn of history, in 1995, 16 December was declared the Day of Reconciliation, and is celebrated each year as a public holiday.

AT THE 'SAFE' HOUSE IN RIVONIA

The peripatetic life of the Black Pimpernel calmed down for a while when Mandela moved to Liliesleaf Farm, 28 acres of land, much of it wooded, in then semi-rural Rivonia, at the northern edge of Johannesburg. On the property was a four-bedroomed, single-storey family home, as well as a number of outbuildings – staff accommodation, workrooms and a thatched cottage.

Architect Arthur Goldreich, his wife, Hazel, and their two young sons were the ostensible inhabitants, but they were a cover for the fact that the farm had, in fact, been bought as an ANC safe house.

At Liliesleaf, Mandela lived as labourer David Motsamayi, doing errands, tending the garden, living in a small outbuilding. He would make tea for the builders and painters who were fixing up the buildings, so low down the social ladder that he was all but invisible even to them. By night, he read avidly about the armed struggles in other countries, in preparation for his own, or sneaked out to meetings, and then went to bed, there to sleep the anxious sleep of the underground freedom fighter.

He was joined by MK recruit Raymond Mhlaba, who was soon to be on his way to China for training, and then by the Communist Party's Michael Harmel. Joe Slovo, Rusty Bernstein and others came for meetings or visits.

Mandela remembered fondly the peaceful weekend visits from the family. While the children played on the farm, he and Winnie stole moments of peace and privacy. He described Liliesleaf as 'more of a sanctuary than a hideout'.

Despite its bucolic air, Liliesleaf was not as safe as it sometimes felt. The illusion of security was shaken by a conversation between two 11-year-old boys, Mandela's son Makgatho and Nicholas Goldreich. Leafing through a copy of *Drum* magazine, Makgatho came upon a picture of Nelson Mandela. 'That's my father,' he exclaimed. Not so, said Nicholas, 'Your father's name is David.' But Makgatho insisted that his father's real name was actually Nelson Mandela.

It was time to move on again. As it happened, Mandela was due to leave the country the next week. In January 1962, he was smuggled across the border to Bechuanaland (now Botswana).

SEEKING AFRICA'S SUPPORT FOR THE STRUGGLE

The steady beating of drums and the rumble of marching feet announced the arrival of 500 armed and uniformed soldiers. As one, they halted to salute His Highness the Emperor of Ethiopia, Haile Selassie, the Lion of Judah.

It was a thrilling sight for Nelson Mandela. Since his teens, he had had a special fascination and admiration for the African nation that fought so hard against colonialism and fascism, and that was the birthplace of African nationalism. And now he was in Ethiopia himself, for the Pan-African Freedom Conference, starting with the parade. 'Here, for the first time in my life, I was witnessing black soldiers, commanded by black generals, applauded by black leaders who were all guests of a black head of state . . . I only hoped it was a vision of what lay in the future for my own country.'

Mandela was there not just as a guest, but as a key speaker at the conference, speaking immediately after the Emperor. He 'flung aside the identity of David Motsamayi and became Nelson Mandela', eloquently outlining the history of the freedom struggle in South Africa and explaining why the decision to enter into the armed struggle had been necessary.

His passionate address was an attempt to persuade the Pan-African Freedom Movement that there was no alternative for the ANC and the liberation struggle but to take up arms. He took his message to African leaders in Tanganyika, Liberia, Ghana, Sierra Leone, Guinea, Algeria, Mali, Morocco, Egypt and Tunisia.

The trip through Africa was significant in many ways. He felt deeply connected to the roots of his Africanness. He experienced a world where African civilisation and culture was celebrated. And he had some success in his goal of drumming up support – training for MK soldiers, and money for weapons.

A CASE OF MISTAKEN IDENTITY

While in Sierra Leone, which had achieved its independence a year earlier, Mandela decided to attend a parliamentary session. He identified himself to the clerk of the House as 'a representative of Chief Luthuli of South Africa'.

The session adjourned and the entire Parliament lined up to shake his hand. He was gratified at the warm and effusive response, but halfway through the receiving line, he realised what was up when one of the parliamentarians said what an honour it was to meet the winner of the Nobel Peace Prize. They thought he was Chief Luthuli!

Mandela immediately informed the clerk of his misunder-standing, but the man was having none of it. It would be too awkward to clear it up, he must continue with the charade. So there he stood, as Chief Luthuli, shaking hands.

When he met the president later, Mandela explained what had happened. It seems there were no hard feelings, as he walked away with a promise of material support for the cause.

MILITARY TRAINING FOR THE MK COMMANDER

For someone heading up an armed wing, Mandela was re-markably unschooled in matters of combat. But now he was to receive military training from the Algerian National Lib-eration Front at bases across the border in Morocco and from the Ethiopian Riot Battalion at Kolfe, outside Addis Ababa.

The Ethiopian programme was intense. He learned to shoot an automatic rifle and a pistol. There was target prac-tice. He was taught to make small bombs and mines, and how to avoid them. There were marches into the country-side, and study sessions with Colonel Tadesse, the assistant commissioner of police.

He was scheduled to have six months of military training, but after just a couple of weeks, there came a telegram from the ANC back home. The armed struggle was escalating, and the presence of the commander of MK was required. Just two months into his military training, Mandela was called back to South Africa. He left with a gift from the colonel – an automatic pistol and 200 rounds of ammunition. That gun is thought to be buried somewhere on Liliesleaf Farm, but, despite extensive searches, it has never been found.

Stopping in Khartoum, he met with the first group of MK recruits headed for Ethiopia for training. Mandela was proud of these young people who had volunteered for the army he was tasked with creating. They had dinner in Addis, and a goat was slaughtered in his honour. The commander of MK was saluted by his soldiers for the first time, and then he returned, via Bechuanaland, to South Africa and Liliesleaf Farm. Fresh from the training and inspiration of his trip, he was ready to push ahead with the armed struggle.

TRAVELLING BOOTS

Nelson Mandela also visited Tanganyika on his 1962 trip through Africa. He was staying with the politician Nsilo Swai and his wife, Vicky Swai, and when he left he had too much luggage – he had to leave behind a suitcase, the contents of which included a pair of brown leather boots. He hoped to pick them up on his way back through the country but it wasn't to be. The Swais ended up keeping the boots for 33 years!

Vicky Swai told the BBC that when they moved from Dar es Salaam to Moshi, near Mount Kilimanjaro, the boots came too. When Nsilo Swai got a job with the United Nations, the boots spent 15 years in New York.

She says: 'I kept them in our bedroom in a cupboard. I never polished them, I never cleaned them but I put newspaper in them to keep them firm. The boots are very strong and the leather is excellent – and when I took them back to Mr Mandela in 1995 they were really like new.'

It might seem a bit odd to keep them so long, and travel with them from place to place, but, she says, 'I really wanted a man who I saw so dedicated to his country to have a memory of these boots.'

The boots still fitted.

CAPTURED!

In the white dust-coat of the servant class, David Motsamayi aka Nelson Mandela took the wheel of Cecil Williams' Austin motorcar. It was a Sunday afternoon and the theatre director and his chauffeur (or, the white MK member and his commander) were leaving Durban for Johannesburg. The

Natal countryside was green and lush, the hills and valleys giving distant glimpses of the Indian Ocean they were leaving behind.

Driving through the midlands, the men admired the scenery and discussed plans for sabotage – the railway alongside the highway seemed a good potential target. As they passed the small town of Cedara, a Ford V8 full of white men shot past them. Mandela turned to see two more cars, similarly packed with white men, coming up behind. He knew instantly that the days of the Black Pimpernel were over. After 17 months on the run, his luck had run out.

Mandela was carrying his loaded revolver. Thoughts of escape crossed his mind, but he and Williams were greatly outnumbered and he knew that if he were to run, it would not end well for him. He slipped his gun and notebook into the upholstery and got out of the car.

As it turned out, roadblocks had been set up all over Natal. Clearly, someone had informed or let slip that Mandela was in Durban. In his cell in Pietermaritzburg he stewed and speculated. Who could it be? Was it a friend, or even a family member, who had betrayed him? Later, the press put it about that white and Indian communists had betrayed him, but many of these troublesome theories were thought to be the work of the Nationalist government trying to sow division between the democrats.

Speculation was futile, he knew. Exhausted, he fell asleep. For this night, at least, he did not have to sleep the fitful sleep of a man on the run. The thing that kept him awake at night had happened. The police had already found him.

COURTROOM DRAMA – AND JAIL TIME

Winnie Mandela, always a striking figure, arrived at the Pretoria courtroom in a traditional beaded headdress and ankle-length skirt – the distinctive attire of the Thembu royal line. Her husband, Nelson Mandela, was the accused in this case, charged with leaving the country illegally and with inciting a strike. When he entered the courtroom that Monday morning in October 1962, instead of his usual well-cut suit and tie, he wore the traditional Xhosa kaross made of leopard skin, the garb of a chief. It was a marvellous piece of symbolism, and when he raised his clenched fist and cried 'Amandla!', the spectators in the public gallery, including the media, rose to their feet. Supporters returned the response: 'Ngawethu!'

It was an electrifying moment. 'I was literally carrying on my back the history, culture and heritage of my people,' he said. The authorities were infuriated and intimidated by this display of African pride and power, by this black man unfazed by the white justice system. The police commander demanded the kaross, or 'blanket', as he called it. Mandela refused to hand it over, telling the colonel that he had no jurisdiction over his clothing, and that if he tried to confiscate it, he would take the case all the way to the Supreme Court. Winnie had been served with a notice from the Minister of Justice that she would be barred from the courtroom if she continued to wear tribal dress. Instead, she wore ANC colours, or the colourful outfits her husband had brought back from his African trip. Other black women came to the trial in their own traditional outfits in solidarity.

The court venue had been changed to Pretoria at the last minute to try and dissuade supporters from holding a mass demonstration at the courthouse. The ANC had organised a Free Mandela campaign, and protests were being held throughout the country. Despite the change of venue, supporters turned up at the court in large numbers to support Nelson Mandela. Outside the court, a praise singer narrated Mandela's genealogy and supporters sang 'Nkosi Sikelel' iAfrika'.

Mandela was given permission to address the court before entering a plea. He used the opportunity to assert that 'this case is a trial of the aspirations of the African people . . .'. He asked the magistrate to recuse himself, saying he did not think a fair trial was possible with a white judge.

The state mustered more than 100 witnesses. Mandela did not dispute that he was guilty of both charges. When the state's case was concluded, Mandela rose. Instead of calling his first witness, he abruptly closed his case.

Nelson Mandela was found guilty.

He used his plea in mitigation to explain to the court how and why he had joined the ANC and the struggle for democracy; that the law was unjust and immoral and that this law had made him a criminal for what he stood for; how the government violence provoked violence; and that he would continue the struggle, no matter what the verdict and sentence.

The sentence was harsh: three years for incitement to strike, two for leaving the country without travel documents. Five years in prison with hard labour and no possibility of parole. The stiffest sentence imposed to date for a political offence. The gallery exploded in song and ululation. He was bundled into the police van and driven away, the strains of 'Nkosi Sikilel' iAfrika' fading away behind him.

MANDELA
THE
PRISONER

TO THE ISLAND

'Green and beautiful, it looked at first more like a resort than a prison,' was how Mandela described his first sight of Robben Island, where he was to see out his five-year sentence. Remote and windswept, the island had been a prison, a leper colony and a lunatic asylum, and was now once again a prison.

Shackled to three other prisoners, he had been driven through the night to Cape Town and put on an old wooden ferry. The men were welcomed with the shout: *'Dis die Eiland! Hier gaan julle vrek!'* (This is the Island. Here you will die!) This set the tone for what was to come – bullying and abuse at the hands of white warders.

He spent just nine months of his five-year sentence there before he was moved to Pretoria Local Prison, in solitary confinement. Nuggets of information filtered through. The news that Harold Wolpe was in detention tipped Mandela off that something had gone wrong. And then he caught a glimpse of Andrew Mlangeni, who was meant to be out of the country on military training. When he saw Thomas Mashifane, the foreman at Liliesleaf, he knew that the authorities must have found the Rivonia hideout.

Later, he heard the details of the raid on Liliesleaf. The dry cleaner's van that made its way down the long driveway. The dozens of policemen and dogs who leapt from the vehicle and found the men around a table, discussing a document – Operation Mayibuye, the blueprint for guerrilla warfare. The search of the property that turned up hundreds of important and incriminating documents.

It was a massive win for the state, and a crippling blow for the ANC, and particularly for MK – the entire High Command had been captured, as Mandela discovered when he was summoned to the prison office. There he found Walter Sisulu, Govan Mbeki, Ahmed Kathrada, Andrew Mlangeni, Bob Hepple, Raymond Mhlaba, Elias Motsoaledi, Denis Goldberg, Rusty Bernstein and James Kantor. They were all charged with sabotage. When they met with their lawyers, Bram Fischer, Vernon Berrangé, Joel Joffe, George Bizos and Arthur Chaskalson, they heard that the state was seeking the death sentence.

The sadistic warders liked to torment the prisoners with the thought of the gallows. There was a rap on Mandela's cell door that night. 'You don't have to worry about sleep,' came the warder's voice. 'You are going to sleep for a long, long time.' To which Mandela replied: 'All of us, you included, are going to sleep for a long, long time.' Brave words, but, as Mandela wrote in his autobiography, it was a small consolation. There was a very real possibility that they would hang.

I CALL ON NELSON MANDELA . . .

It's been described as the trial that changed South Africa, *The State versus the National High Command and Others*. Or, the Rivonia Trial. It opened on 9 October 1963, and to this day many South Africans can quote passages of Nelson Mandela's speech from the dock.

Instead of taking the witness stand, Nelson Mandela, as the first witness, read an opening statement. It was a risky strategy for Mandela. His lawyers warned that it might well jeopardise his legal position – a statement cannot be cross-examined and carries less weight than ordinary testimony. But he and his co-accused decided that it was crucial to give a statement of their politics, and to set the scene for the testimony to follow. He spent two weeks preparing the speech, which is perhaps unequalled in its historic importance in South Africa.

Mandela spoke for nearly five hours. He traced his own history and political development. He admitted to being a founder of MK, and to the military training he had received abroad. He spoke of the readiness of African states to train recruits, and to help financially. He reiterated that he had not planned sabotage recklessly or out of a love for violence, but in response to the years of tyranny, exploitation and oppression of his people.

He painted a vivid picture of the poverty and indignity of the black people of South Africa, the terrible disparities between black and white in every aspect of life. He said that Africans wanted a fair share, equality and justice, and – above all – political rights. Mandela concluded with these words, which have served as a guide and inspiration to fighters for freedom and democracy:

During my lifetime I have dedicated myself to this struggle of the African people. I have fought against white domination, and I have fought against black domination. I have cherished the ideal of a democratic and free society in which all persons live together in harmony and with equal opportunities. It is an ideal which I hope to live for and to achieve. But if needs be, it is an ideal for which I am prepared to die.

Mandela sat down. A long silence fell over the packed courtroom, the tension broken only by the release of breath, a deep collective sigh, and then the sound of women weeping . . .

The speech reverberated around the world. At home, it was printed almost in its entirety in the *Rand Daily Mail*, despite the ban on quoting Mandela's words. This speech, and that final paragraph in particular, came to identify and define him.

THE STATE VS NELSON MANDELA AND OTHERS

On trial with Mandela were Walter Sisulu, secretary-general of the ANC; Denis Goldberg, a Congress of Democrats executive member; Govan Mbeki, a senior ANC official and journalist; Ahmed Kathrada and Lionel Bernstein, both members of the Communist Party; Raymond Mhlaba, Elias Motsoaledi and Andrew Mlangeni, ANC members; and James Kantor, a lawyer. They had all been picked up in the police raid on Liliesleaf farm.

Nelson Mandela, Accused Number One, was already serving a five-year term on Robben Island when the raid took place, but incriminating documents written by him were found at the scene.

In the run-up to the trial, the prisoners were detained under the 90-day law. They were interrogated and kept in solitary confinement. As they were not yet officially charged, the state went to town, whipping up public sentiment against them, portraying them as dangerous revolutionaries, intent on murder and mayhem. At the same time, the United Nations adopted a resolution condemning the government and urging the release of all political prisoners opposing apartheid. Anti-apartheid campaigns kicked into gear.

Locally, supporters demonstrated their solidarity. It was shaping up to be a high-profile trial at home and abroad.

Before the trial even started, Arthur Goldreich and Harold Wolpe bribed a guard and escaped from prison and then successfully evaded capture to skip the country – much to the fury and embarrassment of the state. The state's case suffered another humiliation early on. Bob Hepple, who was released in return for agreeing to turn state's witness, fled the country. Instead of being the prosecution's star witness, he was in Dar es Salaam.

The trial commenced with Bram Fischer leading the defence team, and the arrogant and somewhat overwrought Percy Yutar as lead prosecutor. The charges related to sabotage, promoting communism and soliciting financial help for MK.

Nelson Mandela gave his plea in front of the packed gallery: 'My lord, it is not I, but the Government that should be in the dock today. I plead not guilty.' His co-accused answered similarly. The judge, annoyed, told them he wanted no political speeches; they must plead guilty or not guilty, nothing else.

From the outset, the accused were told by their lawyers to prepare for the worst – there was a good chance they would hang. Their strategy, in the face of a probable death sentence, was to treat it as a political trial, and to conduct themselves with pride and dignity. As Kathrada explains, 'We could not rely on the Appeal Court to overturn a death sentence. Only the struggle and international solidarity would save us from the gallows.'

The prosecution produced 173 witnesses and hundreds of documents and photographs, including Mandela's papers, which had not been destroyed as he had asked, and had been found at Liliesleaf.

On 11 June 1964, Judge Quartus de Wet gave his verdict. Mandela, Sisulu, Goldberg, Mbeki, Mhlaba, Motsoaledi and Mlangeni were convicted on all four counts, Kathrada on three counts. Bernstein was acquitted, to be immediately rearrested and arraigned on other charges. Later he fled the country.

The accused had decided that whatever the verdict or the sentence – even death – they would not appeal. Their lawyers were dismayed, but also admired it as an immensely courageous and politically astute decision. Mandela was prepared for death, and had even made notes for a statement. Point 5 reads: 'If I must die, let me declare for all to know that I will meet my fate like a man.'

The following day, the men were sentenced to life imprisonment. The judge had decided not to impose the death penalty. The relief at dodging the gallows was so intense that the accused actually smiled at the sentence. The courtroom was in chaos – people shouting, running outside with the news, police pushing and shoving. Mandela searched for Winnie and his mother in the crowd but was whisked away, with just enough time to give the ANC salute to spectators.

The police, nervous of the crowd of supporters outside with their banners and their shouts of 'Amandla!', cuffed the convicted men and took them to the cells below, and then into a police van, headed for Pretoria Local. Mandela wrote: 'We could hear the crowd shout "Amandla!" and the slow beautiful rhythms of "Nkosi Sikelel' iAfrika". We made clenched fists through the bars of the window, hoping the crowd could see us, not knowing if they could.'

Chief Albert Luthuli said of the men, at the conclusion of the trial: 'They represent the highest in morality and ethics in the South African political struggle; this morality and ethics has been sentenced to an imprisonment it may never survive. Their policies are in accordance with the deepest international principles of brotherhood and humanity; without their leadership, brotherhood and humanity may be blasted out of existence in South Africa for long decades to come. They believe profoundly in justice and reason; when they are locked away, justice and reason will have departed from the South African scene.'

THE JOKER

During the Rivonia Trial, the bleakness and deprivation of prison life was made tolerable only by the warmth and companionship of friends and comrades. Former Robben Island warder Christo Brand quotes Ahmed Kathrada, speaking in 1993, when he described prison life as 'one of great warmth, fellowship, friendship, humour and laughter, of strong convictions, of a generosity of spirit, solidarity and care'.

There was laughter and joking among the prisoners. The bad-tempered Lieutenant Swanepoel was a good target for mirth. In his autobiography, Mandela recalled how, with Swanepoel watching from the door of the holding cell, Govan Mbeki wrote a note and passed it in a secretive way to Mandela, who read it, nodding seriously, before passing it to Kathy (as Kathrada was known). As Kathy took out his matches and made as if to burn the note, Swanepoel rushed in and grabbed the paper from his hand.

He left the room triumphantly with the scrap of paper, only to return moments later snarling, 'I'll get you for this!'

Mbeki had written in capitals: 'ISN'T SWANEPOEL A FINE LOOKING CHAP?'

ROBBEN ISLAND PRISONER 46664

'You chaps won't be in prison long,' said the warder. 'The demand for your release is too strong. In a year or two you will get out and you will return national heroes. Crowds will cheer you, everyone will want to be your friend, women will want you. Ag, you fellows have it made.'

It was 1964, and Mandela, Sisulu, Mhlaba, Mbeki, Kathrada, Mlangeni and Motsoaledi had been woken in the middle of the night, handcuffed, and hustled out of Pretoria jail and into a police van. Strangely, Mandela recalls the mood as 'not at all sombre' – the friends sang and chanted. The warders gave them cool drinks and sandwiches. And then there was the cheering observation from the warder – which was out by a couple of decades.

The prisoners were taken under heavy police escort to a military airfield and onto a military transport plane.

They were going to Robben Island.

It was here that Mandela was given the prison service number 46664, indicating that he was the 466th prisoner sent to Robben Island in 1964.

Arriving at dawn, they were met by a cold winter wind and tense guards armed with automatic weapons.

The island was isolated and the conditions were harsh. The men were given short khaki pants and jackets, and flimsy jerseys. For bedding, they each had a sisal mat and three thin, worn blankets. Lying down in his cell, Mandela could put his feet against the cold, damp wall of his cell, and touch the opposite wall with his fingertips.

The warder couldn't have been more wrong. Robben Island was to be Mandela's home for 18 years.

TAKING THE STRUGGLE TO THE ISLAND

When they arrived on Robben Island, the political prisoners were immediately put to work breaking rocks in the prison courtyard. Using heavy hammers, Mandela and his fellow inmates pounded stones into gravel, which they then had to transport by wheelbarrow to a skip.

It was back-breaking work that, said ex-political prisoner Neville Alexander, could 'drive the most phlegmatic man into a state of fury. To have to sit in the sun without moving and without being allowed to speak to one's neighbour was hell on earth.'

That first week, prisoners were instructed that the skip had to be half full by the end of the week. They succeeded, and the following week they were told to make it three-quarters full. Again they succeeded. The new order was to fill the skip to the top.

It was clear that the more they did, the more would be demanded of them. The prisoners balked at this and embarked on a go-slow. The guards threatened, but the prisoners persisted.

This protest against work quotas was the first of many such battles. From the outset, Mandela was determined to demand better conditions from the prison authorities, using all the means at the prisoners' disposal – hunger strikes, representations, deputations, protests and court battles.

He wrote: 'I was in a different and smaller arena, an arena for whom the only audience was ourselves and our oppressors. We regarded the struggle in prison as a microcosm of the struggle as a whole. We would fight inside as we had fought outside. The racism and repression were the same; I would simply have to fight on different terms.'

The prison system was intent on breaking the spirit and stripping the prisoners of their dignity. Every victory, no matter how trivial it might seem, was significant. One of the first areas of contestation was clothing. Like many of the rules in prison, those around clothes were discriminatory, and race-based. Black prisoners were given shorts – clothes for boys, not men. Mandela found this 'humiliating', and on the first day of his incarceration demanded long trousers. Two weeks into his prison term, he received a pair of old khaki trousers. He wrote: 'No pin-striped three-piece suit has ever pleased me as much' (which is saying something, for Mandela was a famously stylish dresser).

The pleasure was short-lived. When he discovered that his comrades had not been issued trousers as well, he told the warder to take them back. He wouldn't wear them unless all African prisoners had long trousers.

They got long trousers, eventually. Over the years, the prisoners won many battles, small and large, and continued to fight for their rights – for study privileges, better food, more frequent visits and letters, and access to newspapers (mangled and shredded as they were by the prison censors). But when the leaders arrived on Robben Island, conditions were very harsh. Each tiny cell had a sanitary bucket, which prisoners emptied and washed out every morning. Prisoners showered in cold seawater. As a Group D prisoner – the lowest category, with the fewest privileges – Mandela was allowed to write just one letter and receive one visitor every six months.

Mandela was polite to the warders without being cowed. He made it clear that he expected to be treated properly. Fikile Bam, who served an 11-year term on the Island from 1964 to 1975, said in an interview that Mandela could be quite sharp 'when warders addressed either the group or him, personally, in a rude fashion. He put his foot down immediately telling [them] that that was not the way to treat prisoners, that prisoners were nonetheless people, and they deserved to be treated decently. He did this on almost a daily basis because someone [would] try and mess us around.'

The warder in your section was more important to you than the Minister of Justice, Mandela wrote in his autobiography. He could make your life better in small ways – or make it worse. 'I always tried to be decent to the warders in my section; hostility was usually self-defeating. There was no point in having a permanent enemy among the warders. It was ANC policy to try and educate all people, even our enemies: we believed that all men, even prison service warders, were capable of change, and we did our utmost to try and sway them.'

THE UNIVERSITY IN THE QUARRY

When the Rivonia trialists arrived on the Island, they saw that many political prisoners had had little political education and knew little of the ANC's history. Walter Sisulu began telling them about the movement and its origins. At first, the teaching was informal, but it grew into a two-year course of lectures covering the ANC and the liberation struggle. The curriculum included a course on the history of the Indian struggle, developed and taught by Ahmed Kathrada. There was a course on Marxism, another on the history of the coloured people. And, of course, Mandela's political economy course, tracing the development from early communal societies to feudalism, capitalism and socialism, which he regarded as the most advanced economic model. Inmates who were qualified teachers formed RITA, the Robben Island Teachers' Association, and tutored other prisoners in a range of subjects – even German.

The teaching was done through questions and answers and debate. The 'classroom' was the limestone quarry where the prisoners worked.

Soon, word got out to the general prisoners, who wanted

to learn too. A sort of correspondence course was developed, with lecture notes smuggled to the general section, and questions and comments coming back to the teachers.

Mandela wrote in his autobiography that the leaders and teachers learned from the prisoners, most of whom had little formal education, but who were quick to ask what the theory and philosophy meant in practice. He found their questions immensely valuable, as they forced the leaders to think hard about their views.

As well as informal studying, many political prisoners were enrolled in formal education through correspondence colleges. Studying was a privilege on Robben Island, not a right. The authorities could grant or revoke permission at will. Group D prisoners didn't have that right, but within months of arriving on the Island, Mandela and his cohort were told that they could apply for permission. Soon, just about all of them were studying for one degree or another.

Many prisoners earned multiple degrees. Dikgang Moseneke, who went on to become Deputy Chief Justice in the new South Africa, obtained his matric, a BA and a BJuris degree while on Robben Island. During his 26 years in prison, Ahmed Kathrada earned four university degrees: a BA, a BLib and two BA Honours degrees. He wanted to read for a master's degree, but honours degrees were as high as prisoners were allowed to go.

Robben Island was known as 'The University'. As well as being a site of incarceration and deprivation, the Island was, for many, an extraordinary opportunity for personal growth and transformation. It was here that many struggle stalwarts received or sharpened their political education, and a new generation of young leaders was forged.

Not all debate had to do with the liberation struggle. One topic that came up repeatedly was whether or not there were tigers in Africa. Some claimed to have seen them with their own eyes. Some pointed out that there was an isiXhosa word for tiger, different from the word for leopard. Others maintained that, no, tigers were found only in Asia, not in Africa.

HOLDING THE BABY

Of the many indignities and deprivations that prisoners were subjected to, one of the very worst was being denied access to their family members, particularly in times of family stress, grief or celebration.

Christo Brand, a prison warder on Robben Island who knew Mandela well, tells a remarkable tale.

One day, some years into Nelson Mandela's prison term, Winnie arrived, as she always did, on the ferry to Robben Island. Black visitors had to sit on the top deck and Winnie was dressed appropriately for this uncomfortable passage, wrapped in a blanket against the cold and rain.

Brand met her at the embarkation point, where bags were

searched, and accompanied her to the visitors' centre. There she took off the blanket to reveal – a baby! Brand recalled: 'Now I was faced with this extraordinary situation. Winnie was holding out a baby to me. What on earth was I meant to do? I told her: "Mrs Mandela, you must leave the baby with the other visitors in the waiting room while you see your husband."'

She did as she was told and went into the visitor's booth alone, pressing her hand against her husband's hand, the thick glass panel between them. She told him that she had managed to get their four-month-old granddaughter Zoleka, the daughter of Zindzi, into the prison, Nelson asked Brand if he could please let him see the child. Brand refused his pleas and those of Winnie, knowing that he would lose his job and Mandela all his privileges.

Brand wrote: 'It was a flesh-and-blood moment when your heart told you it was only human to find a way around the cruelty.'

Brand asked to hold the baby while Winnie made arrangements for the next visit. He took the tiny child into the booth where Mandela was sitting, the window now closed, and handed him the baby.

'He took her and held her and he just said, "Oh", and I saw tears in his eyes as he kissed the baby. We both stood in silence and after about 30 seconds he knew he must hand her back to me.'

The stakes were so high for both prisoner and warder that

they knew it would have to be their secret, even from Winnie. Brand says, 'We became allies for life without referring to that day again all the time he was in prison.'

KNOW YOUR ENEMY . . .

Nelson Mandela learned to understand and speak Afrikaans during his time on Robben Island. At this time, Afrikaans was regarded as the language of the white minority, the language of the oppressors. The 1976 Soweto uprising was prompted by just this issue – the forced introduction of Afrikaans as the language of instruction in schools. Many activists on Robben Island at the time despised the language, and some were offended by his interest in it and willingness to learn.

Fikile Bam, who was on the Island with Mandela, described in an interview: 'Nelson was very serious about his Afrikaans, and not just the language, but he was very serious about learning to understand the Afrikaner – his mind and how he thought. Because in his mind, and he actually preached this, the Afrikaner was an African. He belonged to the soil and whatever solution there was going to be on the political issues, was going to involve Afrikaans people . . . He had absolutely no qualms about greeting people in Afrikaans, and about trying his Afrikaans out on the warders.'

Many years later, when Mandela was in Victor Verster

Prison, his last stop before freedom, he made an arrange-
ment with Warrant Officer Swart, who was his cook and
general helper. Swart, who was keen to improve his English,
would speak to Mandela in that language. Mandela would
speak to Swart in Afrikaans. That way, they both improved
their weaker language, and helped the other improve his.

His study of the language, history, traditions and culture
of Afrikaans South Africans stood him in good stead with
the warders on Robben Island and of course later, when he
engaged with the Nationalist government in talks about
talks, and then negotiations, and finally in the Government
of National Unity. Later still, Mandela's deep understanding
of the importance of certain symbols and cultural practices
led to one of the key nation-building moments in post-
apartheid history – the 1995 Rugby World Cup final.

COLD COMFORT AND ICY SHOWERS

Early on in Mandela's incarceration on the Island, an
international authority on prisons came to look at the
conditions. The prisoners were given new uniforms and, on
the morning of the visitor's arrival, taken to another section
of the prison where the showers worked, and where they
could properly clean themselves for the first time.

Mandela told their esteemed visitor that he should come

and visit more often, as they'd not only been given new clothes but had also been allowed to take a shower.

The visitor went on his way, reporting that the conditions weren't too bad and that he was fairly sure that no atrocities would be permitted. The prisoners were punished for Mandela's outspokenness, though. Kathrada describes the 'typically vindictive' response from the warders: 'The very next morning, in the middle of winter and with rain bucketing down, the warders woke us at 5.30, yelling that since we wanted so badly to bath, they were going to let us do so.

'They took us to the old section of the prison and made us all take ice-cold showers. No one was excused. This "punishment" was repeated for days.'

@~@

LETTERS FROM INSIDE

In the Cachalia household, the postman brought not just the usual round of bills, letters and circulars. On occasion, there would be a letter from Nelson Mandela in prison.

Yusuf and Amina Cachalia were fellow activists and close friends of Mandela's. Although Mandela had gone to prison when their son Ghaleb was a boy, leaving him with just scattered recollections of the man, he remembers the stir that a letter would bring.

'There was a long period of correspondence between my mother and Nelson,' says Ghaleb. 'From time to time a letter would arrive and that would be a great excitement for all of us. My parents would read it carefully, looking for its hidden meaning, and then they would share it with my sister and me. Mandela would often refer to us children and ask about us.'

The absent Mandela loomed large and featured strongly in their family folklore, and Ghaleb grew up hearing stories about him. A particular favourite was the story of the dinner that Yusuf and Nelson cooked in honour of Amina's 21st birthday. The two men – not exactly Jamie Olivers in the kitchen – spent the whole afternoon in a comrade's flat, preparing and roasting 21 pigeons. It was a kind and rather dramatic gesture, but as a meal it was a disaster – the celebrant took one look at the little brown birds and felt immediately queasy. She made do with a bit of rice and gravy for supper.

HEARTBREAKING NEWS FROM HOME

A one-line telegram gave prisoner Nelson Mandela devastating news – his oldest son, Thembi Mandela, was dead. At just 25, and the father of two young children, he had been killed in a car accident.

Mandela took to his cell, lay on his bed and thought about his son. When he didn't emerge for supper, Sisulu came and knelt by the bed. Mandela handed him the telegram and his old friend held his hand in silence.

'I do not have words to express the sorrow, or the loss I felt. It left a hole in my heart that can never be filled,' Mandela wrote of his son's death. The grief was exacerbated by the authorities' refusal to allow him to attend his son's funeral. He could not lay the young man's spirit to rest, as a father should. Nor could he comfort the suffering family beyond a letter to Evelyn.

This loss came just a year after another: the death of Mandela's mother. Then, too, he had been refused permission to attend the funeral. Then, too, he confronted the hard fact that his commitment to the struggle came at great cost to his family.

These losses were hard to bear, and long-lasting. In 2012, when researchers at the Nelson Mandela Centre of Memory unearthed an article in the *Cape Argus* about the accident, Thembi's daughter Ndileka Mandela said: 'Whenever I ask Granddad about Dad I always see the pain that is still etched in his eyes. He always has this faraway look a person has when they reminisce and he says very little save to say that Thembi was a very responsible young man,' she said. 'One can see how the apartheid system did irreparable pain by denying him the basic human right of saying farewell and paying last respects to one's dearly departed. The pain of not being able to bury his first-born son will never be erased.'

'HERE YOU ARE AMONGST FRIENDS'

Ronnie Mamoepa was a teenager when he was sentenced to five years on Robben Island. In a television interview, he described how he and his young comrades, who were arrested after the Soweto uprising in 1976, went to the Island looking forward to meeting Nelson Mandela, 'this giant of our people'.

He tells the story: 'A month later we were working in front of the reception area – and there they came. Madiba, Walter Sisulu, Kathrada, Mlangeni, Motsoaledi, Toivo ja Toivo. All. They came from the football ground and they came to us and shook our hands, one by one. They were very humble people.'

The older prisoners looked out for the new arrivals. 'Each time you met Mandela or Sisulu, they always asked, "Are they writing to you from home? Do they come and visit you?" They were always concerned for our well-being.'

Lionel Davis, who was on the Island from 1964 to 1971, speaks of Mandela's care for new arrivals: 'When you arrived on the island, the warders would go out of their way to humiliate the new prisoner. They would strip you naked, or take away your shoes and make you walk on the broken-up slate. They liked to see your discomfort, especially in that section, with educated people, and the troublemakers.

'Nelson Mandela was very caring, him and Walter Sisulu. He would see when prisoners were uncomfortable. Mandela would notice your discomfort, and had the ability to calm you down. He would say, "Here you are amongst friends." This was not an ANC thing or a PAC thing, this was a humane thing.'

FAMILY PHOTOS

In the early 1970s, Nelson Mandela received a marvellous gift – a photograph album, made by his wife, Winnie, and filled with pictures of his family. Prison authorities had decided to allow prisoners to receive photographs of immediate family members. Nelson cherished the album, carefully pasting in additional pictures as he got them, looking lovingly at his wife and children, and then at the grandchildren he had never met or held.

One of the prisoners in his section asked to borrow the album, and Mandela obliged. Then someone else asked. And someone else. Word spread that Mandela had an album, and he got requests from further afield, Sections F and G. These men rarely received letters, let alone photographs, and, as Mandela put it, 'it seemed ungenerous to deny them this window on the world'. The precious album was soon in tatters, and sometimes photographs were removed.

Others would ask for a photograph, rather than the whole album, Ronnie Mamoepa recalled in an interview: 'Many political prisoners will attest that Madiba's family photos were given to a whole range of us. If you asked Tata, "Can we have a photo of Ma Winnie?" he would always give you.'

THE MYSTERY OF THE MANUSCRIPT

Nelson Mandela woke to the sound of digging. The noise seemed to be coming from the courtyard. Peering out, he saw a work crew taking picks and shovels to the hard earth. This was potentially disastrous – there was something there he really did not want them to find . . .

Sometime earlier, Ahmed Kathrada and Walter Sisulu had suggested that Mandela write his autobiography, to be published on his upcoming 60th birthday. Their hope was that it would keep the idea of the struggle alive and inspire young people, at a time when the press was being silenced by bans and restrictions, and the law prohibited any mention of the ANC or its leaders in the South African press.

Mandela's famous work ethic kicked into gear, and he worked on the manuscript for hours every night. In the morning, he would pass his writing on to Kathy, who would review it, read it to Sisulu, and write their comments in the margin. Laloo Chiba would then condense the revised text into his microscopic shorthand. Ten full pages of Mandela's writing would fit onto a small piece of paper, which would be given to Mac Maharaj, whose task it was to smuggle it out.

The transcribed manuscript was hidden in the binding of the textbooks Mac used for his studies. Once it was safely delivered, the original manuscript would be destroyed. But what to do with 500 pages in the meantime?

The prisoners decided to bury it in the garden in the courtyard. They divided the manuscript in three, wrapped each section in plastic and placed it in an empty cocoa tin. Using sharpened iron stakes as digging tools, Kathy, Sisulu, Eddie Daniels and Mandela went to work. The bigger tin, containing the larger portion of the manuscript, was lodged in a space carved out under a drainpipe. The two smaller tins were buried in more shallow spots.

Imagine the alarm, then, when the prisoners heard the sound of digging, and saw a work crew digging foundations for a wall – right where the manuscript was buried.

At breakfast time, drums of porridge were wheeled into the courtyard. The warders ordered the workers out of the yard, to prevent their having contact with the prisoners. Mandela and the others had their chance. They wandered casually over to the place where they had buried their treasure, and saw that the foundation trench was right where the two smaller containers were buried. As inconspicuously as possible, they started digging. Fortunately, they unearthed the two smaller containers easily, and slipped the contents into their shirts. To dig up the larger container from its deeper hiding place would have taken too long. They had to take the chance that the builders would not need to dislodge the pipe in order to build the wall.

When Mandela returned from the quarry later that day, he was greeted by a distressing sight – the pipe had been dug up. There was no way they'd not found the manuscript. Sure enough, the next morning he was summoned to see the commanding officer. They'd found the manuscript and recognised his handwriting, as well as Sisulu's and Kathrada's notes in the margin. The punishment was harsh – the men had abused their study privileges, so those privileges would now be suspended indefinitely. It was to be four years before they were reinstated.

Meanwhile, when Mac was released from prison in 1976, he was able to smuggle the manuscript out and send it to England. He spent six months working with a typist and reconstructing the manuscript, a copy of which he gave to Oliver Tambo in Lusaka. It wasn't published while Mandela was in prison. Years later, he wrote *Long Walk to Freedom*, based on the work he had done night after night on Robben Island, and hidden – unsuccessfully as it turned out – in the garden in the prison courtyard.

ROBBEN ISLAND SHAKESPEARE

From his student days at the University of Natal, Sonny Venkatrathnam was intrigued by Shakespeare's plays. When he was found guilty of terrorism and imprisoned on Robben Island in 1972, he asked his wife to send him a copy of *The Complete Works of Shakespeare* to keep him company during the 12 long years he was to spend there.

In the unpredictable way of the prison system, the rules changed at some point, and prisoners were allowed only religious books. Shakespeare was confiscated, and relegated to the storeroom.

One Sunday morning Venkatrathnam told the warder on duty that his Bible, by William Shakespeare, was locked in the storeroom. The warder let him take the book. Once he had it back in his possession, Venkatrathnam disguised the book by covering the front, back and spine with the Diwali greeting cards his family sent him. When warders asked what it was, he told them it was his Bible.

In anticipation of his release from the Island, Venkatrathnam asked his comrades to sign his 'Bible' next to their favourite passages. Thirty-three prisoners signed it, including Mac Maharaj, Walter Sisulu, Nelson Mandela,

Govan Mbeki and Ahmed Kathrada, making it probably the most remarkable 'autograph book' in the world.

Mandela's signature and the date, 16 December 1977, appears in blue beside a passage from *Julius Caesar*:

Cowards die many times before their deaths.
The valiant never taste of death but once.
Of all the wonders that I yet have heard,
It seems to me most strange that men should fear,
Seeing that death, a necessary end,
Will come when it will come.

It was a passage that Mandela often repeated.

THE PRISONERS PLAN THEIR ESCAPE

Was there ever a prisoner who didn't harbour dreams of escape? For the political prisoners on Robben Island, there were many plans and schemes over the years, and one occasion when Mandela came very close to an attempt.

It was Mac Maharaj's idea. He had been to visit a dentist on the mainland, and noticed that there was an open window in the surgery, with a short drop to the street outside. The plan was simple: Mac and Mandela would apply to visit the dentist, and, once there, they would jump out the window.

The two men put in for a dentist visit. The day came, and they were taken off the Island to Cape Town. In the dentist's office, their handcuffs were taken off, and it looked as if the plan might actually work. But when Mac and Mandela looked out the window, the street was suspiciously deserted. Was it a trap? Had the police got wind of their plan? Perhaps they would take the opportunity to shoot Mandela as he fled, and thus rid themselves of this troublesome man.

The plan was abandoned. They headed back to the Island, their teeth, presumably, in good shape. We'll never know whether they might have made good their escape, and, if they had, how differently the history of South Africa might have turned out.

MANDELA
THE
NEGOTIATOR

TO A DIFFERENT PRISON

One April day in 1982, a delegation of prison officials came into Nelson Mandela's cell and told him to pack up his things. He was being transferred. After 18 years on the Island, Mandela was leaving, for who-knew-where. Walter Sisulu, Raymond Mhlaba and Andrew Mlangeni received the same order but no further information.

It took just half an hour to pack their meagre possessions of nearly two decades into a few boxes, and, without even the opportunity to say goodbye to their friends and comrades, they were soon on the ferry to Cape Town. Mandela described in his autobiography how unsettling it was, leaving after so long. The Island wasn't home, but it was known and, in a sense, comfortable. And he had no idea where he was going next.

When they reached the mainland, the men were bundled into a windowless truck that drove for an hour through suburbs and vineyards and deposited them, in the dark, in front of the formidable gates of a security facility. They had arrived at Pollsmoor Prison.

They were left to speculate as to the reasons for their being there. Why had they been moved? What were the authorities up to? Were they trying to reduce their influence on the younger political prisoners? Was it some sort of gesture to diminish the powerful symbolism of Robben Island in the struggle?

The four men were given a spacious top-floor room with proper beds and bedding, showers and toilets. There was a small terrace and an outdoor section where they could walk during the day and see the blue sky and a glimpse of the Constantiaberg mountains. Conditions were, in many ways, better than they were used to. They were given meat and vegetables instead of pap, and received *The Guardian* and *Time* magazine. They had a radio and there was a television and videos (new to them – television had been introduced in 1976, and video was relatively recent).

Mandela struggled to adjust. The prison was all dark corridors and clanging cells and concrete – no view, no grass – and the cells were damp and cold. Although they were now on the mainland, they were in some ways more isolated than they had been on that windswept island 12 kilometres out to sea. They were the only political prisoners in the facility (Ahmed Kathrada arrived some months later) and were kept separate from the common prisoners. There was none of the camaraderie of Robben Island, and they missed the debates and discussion.

Restrictions on letters and visits were loosening, and Mandela was able to correspond broadly – with clerics, old friends, family members, possible allies and influential members of various constituencies. Still, it was enormously frustrating being cut off from the dramatic events of the early 1980s. PW Botha's Tricameral Parliament, designed to co-opt Indian and coloured South Africans. The launch of the United Democratic Front (UDF). The growing spirit of defiance. The escalation of violence.

Pollsmoor did, however, provide Mandela with a diversion that gave him much pleasure – a garden. He received permission to plant vegetables, as he had on Robben Island, but on a much grander scale. In 16 oil drums, each cut in half and filled with good soil, he grew carrots, broccoli and other vegetables – 900 plants, at one point. In a straw hat and gloves, he spent hours a day working in his garden, and produced a great bounty that was shared with the warders. Every Sunday he provided the prison kitchen with vegetables to make a special meal for the common-law prisoners. Mandela often described himself as a country boy at heart, with a country boy's love of the outdoors, the earth and its plants – even if these plants were on the roof of a prison, in half an oil drum.

THE POWER OF TOUCH

Imagine the desolation of knowing no loving human touch for decades. No goodnight kiss. No brushing of fingers.

No warm embrace. This, of course, is the life of a long-term prisoner.

When Nelson Mandela had been at Pollsmoor for two years, instead of being led to the normal visiting area for the scheduled family visit, he was taken to a small room with just a table in it. Warrant Officer James Gregory returned with Winnie, their daughter Zeni and Zeni's youngest daughter.

Mandela wrote poignantly of this moment in his auto-biography: 'Before either of us knew it, we were in the same room and in each other's arms. I kissed and held my wife for the first time in all these many years. It was a moment I had dreamed about a thousand times. It was as if I were still dreaming. I held her to me for what seemed like an eternity. We were still and silent except for the sound of our hearts. I did not want to let go of her at all, but I broke free and embraced my daughter and then took her child onto my lap. It had been twenty-one years since I had even touched my wife's hand.'

CRACKERS FOR CHRISTMAS

It is well known that Nelson Mandela's personal warmth was pretty much irresistible.

In 1988, he was diagnosed with tuberculosis, a potentially devastating lung condition, no doubt exacerbated by the damp prison conditions he'd lived in for decades. Mandela spent three months in his own ward in a private clinic (a state hospital was considered too risky – it would have been almost impossible to keep his presence under wraps).

He was the first black patient the private hospital had ever treated. And likely the most popular. He had the nurses charmed from the start, and they fell over themselves to bring him treats. It was here that he tasted pizza for the first time.

The nurses wanted to take him to their Christmas party, but regulations could only be stretched so far. Undeterred, they had their own little celebration in his ward, bringing turkey and trimmings to him.

And what's a Christmas celebration without Christmas crackers? They had those, too. But this was pushing the boundaries. The warders responsible for Mandela's security opened each cracker, checked it and put it back together again before the guest of honour and his companions could pull them.

ALMOST FREE

As early as 1985, Mandela had a shot at freedom. The Nationalist government was eager to get the headline-making Mandela out of jail – but on their own terms. They would

release Mandela and other political prisoners who 'unconditionally rejected violence as a political instrument'. It
was not the first time this offer had been made, but with
violence sweeping the country, the imposition of the first
of two States of Emergency, and the pressure coming
from abroad, there was a renewed eagerness on the part of
the government.

President PW Botha declared in Parliament that he would
free all political prisoners on that condition. He claimed,
disingenuously: 'It is therefore not the South African government which stands in the way of Mr Mandela's freedom.
It is he himself.'

It must have been heartbreaking for the prisoners, after all
these years, to be in sight of freedom. We can only imagine
the temptation to negotiate on this basis. Or any basis. But
Mandela – and his comrades on Robben Island – were resolute. He refused this conditional freedom.

At a UDF rally at Soweto's Jabulani Stadium, his daughter Zindzi delivered the words that her father had written,
the first words of his that the people had legally heard in
20 years. He reiterated his commitment to the ANC and its
struggle, and challenged Botha to renounce violence. To
unban the ANC. To free political prisoners.

It is a marvellous speech, moving and resolute, which ends
with these words: 'Only free men can negotiate. Prisoners
cannot enter into contracts . . . I cannot and will not give
any undertaking at a time when I and you, the people,

are not free. Your freedom and mine cannot be separated. I will return.'

The crowd was ecstatic. Botha, however, was livid. He had made his announcement in Parliament and on national radio, and yet this upstart prisoner was refusing to play ball. He went on television to say that he would never give in to Mandela.

Denis Goldberg, the only white Rivonia trialist in prison, accepted the conditional offer of release. He had been held in isolation in Pretoria Central Prison for 22 years. The very apartheid system that he was jailed for fighting against ensured that he was held separately from his black comrades.

Mandela was understanding of Goldberg's position. He maintained that being apart from his friends was a dreadful hardship, that Goldberg had suffered terribly in his solitary state, and that it was time for him to go to his family.

READY TO TALK ABOUT TALKS?

Out of the blue, Mandela was informed that he would no longer be living in the Pollsmoor 'penthouse' with Sisulu, Mlangeni, Mhlaba and Kathrada. Instead, he was moved into a new cell on the ground floor with three rooms and a separate toilet. The facilities were better – if dank and cheerless – but he missed his colleagues and his garden. And besides, he couldn't work out what the state was up to. Why was he separated from the others? Why the new accommodation?

Of course, there were no answers from the authorities, but, whatever their reasons, he decided to put his new-found solitude to good use. For some time, he had been considering the idea of dialogue with the government. Perhaps, in his privacy and isolation, he could now find a way to take a step in that direction. It was a delicate situation. Both sides viewed discussions with the other as weakness, as betrayal. The government maintained their position that they wouldn't talk to terrorists and communists. And the ANC would not talk to the racist, repressive government until they unbanned the ANC, released political prisoners and pulled the troops from the townships.

Mandela believed, though, that however tricky and sensitive the situation, dialogue was the best – perhaps the only – way to push the struggle for democracy forward. Without it, the future seemed to hold only continued violence, bloodshed and repression.

A further complication was that a move in this direction should, by rights, have been made by the ANC leadership in Lusaka. But of course Mandela was not able to discuss his plans and ideas with Oliver Tambo. He decided that this was one of those times in which a leader must take the lead in a new direction. Nelson Mandela was going to move in the direction of negotiating with the Nationalist government.

HAPPY BIRTHDAY TO YOU . . .

When Nelson Mandela turned 70 in 1988, the Brits threw him a mega birthday party. More than 74 000 well-wishers packed London's Wembley Stadium, while 83 top stars of the pop and rock world performed. The party went on for 12 hours, but the celebrant himself was, of course, still incarcerated in Pollsmoor Prison.

Producer and impresario Tony Hollingsworth first developed the idea of a Mandela tribute event after talking to Jerry Dammers of The Specials. Dammers had written the hit single 'Free Nelson Mandela' in 1984, and was a founder of Artists Against Apartheid. In 1987, Hollingsworth met with Archbishop Trevor Huddleston, president of Britain's Anti-Apartheid Movement. Writing in *The Daily Telegraph*, he says that he sought to reformulate the ANC's message: 'In my view, the way they were presented to the public – as protesters in the street – could only appeal to a small percentage of the world's population. If they were to appeal more broadly we had to reposition them as positive and confident. I thought their main communications problem was that many TV and radio news organisations around the world were still referring to Nelson Mandela . . . as a "Black Terrorist Leader", and while a "Black Leader" could

113

be released from prison, a "Black Terrorist Leader" could not.' And he had a proposal – a tribute concert.

Hollingsworth's strategy was clear and ambitious: to call for Mandela's release, which he saw as the first step to ending apartheid, and to produce the tribute not just as a concert but as a global broadcast event. Even before the Anti-Apartheid Movement came on board, he took the leap and booked Wembley Stadium for 11 June 1988, a month before Mandela's 70th birthday.

Then Hollingsworth set about trying to get the biggest names in music to commit to his concert, starting with Dire Straits, then at the peak of their popularity, and a band that he thought likely to lure the global broadcasters. It wasn't an easy task. No one said no, exactly, but everyone was waiting to see who else would commit before they did . . .

And when one or two did, everyone else followed. All the greats were there: Dire Straits, Simple Minds, George Michael, Whitney Houston, UB40, Aswad, Natalie Cole, Sly and Robbie, Youssou N'Dour, Phil Collins, the Bee Gees, Sting, Tracy Chapman, Stevie Wonder, Eurythmics, Miriam Makeba and Hugh Masekela, and many more – 83 acts in all. Peter Gabriel sang his famous anthem, 'Biko'.

It was a day that none of the performers – or the audience – will ever forget. And, in living rooms the world over, 600 million people got a taste of the vibe, and a little bit of the Mandela magic. The television audience was, at the time, the largest ever for an entertainment event.

It wasn't all peace, love and understanding. Both the Anti-Apartheid Movement and Hollingsworth received bomb threats. Fox Television cut out some of the more political moments. But the Nelson Mandela Birthday Tribute Concert was a massive success, raising worldwide awareness around his imprisonment. It would not be too grand a claim to say that this London birthday party played a significant role in putting pressure on the apartheid regime to move more quickly in the direction of releasing Nelson Mandela.

LAST STOP ON THE ROAD TO FREEDOM

The move towards freedom continued. Mandela was once again ushered to a new abode without notice or explanation. The head of Pollsmoor Prison arrived one evening at the hospital, where Mandela was being treated for tuberculosis, and told him to get ready to leave. He was to put on his new civilian clothes and his dressing gown and slip out, along with warder Christo Brand (who was likewise in the dark as to their destination).

Brand followed a speeding, unmarked police car through the night. Was Mandela being released? They weren't heading to Pollsmoor. Where could they be going?

An hour later they arrived at Victor Verster Prison, in the pretty winemaking country near Paarl. Here Mandela was allocated a simple single-storey cottage with three bedrooms, a pool and a treed garden. And, of course, a high wall topped with razor wire.

It was December 1988, and this was to be his last stop on the road to freedom, a kind of halfway place between prison and the real world. He was no longer bound by the rules and schedules of incarceration – he could eat and sleep and swim and walk as and when he liked. This personal freedom was a lovely feeling after years of having his time and movements controlled – but he was in prison, nonetheless.

For company, he had a warder-turned-cook, Warrant Officer Swart, who had been on Robben Island. Swart would make Mandela's meals, which the prisoner could warm up in a microwave. This appliance was, of course, entirely new to Mandela, having been introduced during the period of his incarceration, and was a source of some fascination.

Swart was flustered by Mandela's insistence on doing the dishes after the meal. The prisoner felt it was only fair; after all, Swart had done the cooking. Neither did he approve of Mandela's making his own bed every morning.

Swart made another contribution, which visitors appreciated. Mandela was not a drinker, and would only take the occasional sip of sweet wine. Swart bought the wine that Mandela preferred, but balked at serving it to visitors. When George Bizos was due for lunch, Swart proposed buying two bottles of wine – the sweet wine Mandela liked, but which Swart considered 'cheap stuff and not very nice', and a decent dry white. Mandela was sure that Bizos would neither know the difference nor care. It turned out he was wrong – Bizos chose the dry!

In his autobiography, Mandela remembered fondly his 71st birthday. His wife, children and grandchildren – almost the entire family – gathered at his cottage to celebrate. It was the first time he had been together with them all. It was a marvellous occasion, ably catered by Swart, and Mandela described both the 'deep, deep pleasure' he felt and the pain of knowing how much he had missed, for so long.

FREEDOM FOR SOME

In September 1989, FW de Klerk was sworn in as president, and made it known that he was willing to talk peace. Mandela renewed his own offer to talk.

And then came a sudden and unexpected announcement – Ahmed Kathrada, Raymond Mhlaba, Andrew Mlangeni and Walter Sisulu were to be released. In his book, warder Christo Brand described the elation and celebration in prison, and commented: 'Even some of my hardline colleagues looked happy and relieved for these old-timers who had been so suddenly set free.'

On 15 October 1989, they were officially released in Johannesburg. Mandela was delighted for his friends. De Klerk was going some way to meeting the ANC's demands; he released the men unconditionally, with no bans. He'd also started dismantling some of the demeaning and inhuman building blocks of apartheid, the racial segregation of facilities such as parks, buses, libraries and beaches.

Mandela's closest comrades and his companions of decades had finally been released from prison, but they were still a long way from real freedom. The ANC was still banned, for instance. And the National Party was still attached to the idea of protecting 'group rights', which seemed to many like simply trying to preserve white domination. Nonetheless, it was clear that De Klerk was prepared to listen, understand, consider and negotiate, which in itself was a real departure from his predecessors.

Mandela remained convinced that real negotiation could not begin until the ANC and other organisations were unbanned and political prisoners released. When he met with De Klerk, he reiterated his position – that he would not agree to his own release until the ANC was unbanned. If the conditions in the outside world had not changed – the State of Emergency in place, the ANC banned, political prisoners in jail – he would be working for a banned organisation, doing the same things he went to jail for. 'You must simply rearrest me after I walk through those gates,' he said.

Until then, he was to stay in Victor Verster.

AT LAST! ANC UNBANNED, MANDELA TO BE FREED

Things began to move quickly as the 1980s ended and the new decade began. It was becoming increasingly evident even to the National Party that the situation was untenable. Successive States of Emergency had failed to quell unrest at home, and internationally the country was increasingly isolated economically, through sanctions, as well as culturally. Pressure was building.

On 2 February 1990, De Klerk announced in Parliament that the ANC, the PAC, the SACP and over 30 other political groups were to be unbanned. Political prisoners were to be released. The State of Emergency was lifted. The death penalty was suspended. And Nelson Mandela was to be released. It was a truly momentous announcement. De Klerk was finally preparing to end decades of white minority rule and move towards democracy. Archbishop Desmond Tutu said at the time: 'He has taken my breath away.'

Some days after the announcement in Parliament that the ANC was unbanned and political prisoners were to be released, Mandela was summoned to a meeting at Tuynhuys. There, De Klerk informed him that he was to be released the next day. Although there had been much speculation that his release was imminent, nonetheless it came as a surprise.

Mandela, who had waited 27 years for this moment, replied – to De Klerk's astonishment – that he wanted to spend ten more days at Victor Verster, so that the ANC and the Mandela family would have time to prepare for his release.

But De Klerk had made already plans – Mandela would be flown to Johannesburg and escorted to the Union Buildings in Pretoria. There, on the balcony, he would be presented to the country by De Klerk.

De Klerk may have had his plan, but Mandela had his own. He would not be flying to Johannesburg. He would not be told how and when he could leave prison.

Mandela wrote in his autobiography: 'I wanted to walk out of the gates of Victor Verster and be able to thank those who looked after me and greet the people of Cape Town. Though I was from Johannesburg, Cape Town had been my home for nearly 30 years. I would make my way back to Johannesburg, but when I chose to, not when the government wanted me to.'

He told De Klerk: 'Once I am free, I will look after myself.'

By all accounts, the president was angry at this unexpected stand by the prisoner. Something of a compromise was reached. Mandela relented on the ten-day delay – De Klerk had already informed the foreign press that the release would take place the next day – but he would walk out of Victor Verster a free man.

MANDELA
WALKS
FREE

.

HIS FIRST WALK TO FREEDOM

They say that Americans of a certain age remember where they were when they saw Neil Armstrong walk on the Moon. Very many South Africans – this writer included – remember watching Nelson Mandela's release. But first, the long wait in front of the television. Where was he? Why was he late? What was happening?

And then there he was, tall and stately and grey-haired, coming through the gates of Victor Verster Prison, hand in hand with Winnie. The first public sighting of him in nearly three decades. At 4.22 pm, on 11 February 1990, Nelson Mandela was free at last after 27 years of imprisonment.

'Long live . . .' shouted the crowd, 'Long live . . .'

We now know that the day was chaotically busy and frenetic. Winnie and Walter and other colleagues arriving on a chartered flight from Johannesburg. People coming and going. Endless phone calls. Mandela's belongings being packed into crates. The farewell visits from warders, and a celebratory air. It was actually happening.

The calm centre of this mayhem was Nelson Mandela himself, quietly writing his speech, consulting occasionally with colleagues – Trevor Manuel, Valli Moosa and Cyril

123

Ramaphosa were there – preparing to address his country-men at last.

And then it was time.

Mandela's first moments of freedom were a taste of what was to come. He walked out of the prison expecting to be greeted by the warders and their families, come to say goodbye. He had seriously underestimated his reception. A frantic metallic clicking sound greeted him before he even reached the gate. It was the sound of the cameras wielded by a huge international press corps desperate to capture that historic moment.

And we all know that picture. Nelson and Winnie, hold-ing hands, smiling broadly, each greeting the crowd with their free hand raised in a fist.

A HERO ADDRESSES THE NATION

After manoeuvring through the crowds outside Victor Ver-ster Prison, Mandela's driver soon found the roads blocked by the throngs making their way to the Cape Town City Hall. An estimated quarter of a million people had been gathering on the Grand Parade since that morning, and the streets were almost impossible to navigate.

They couldn't get to the Grand Parade. The crowd envel-oped the car, people hammering excitedly on the roof. In the pandemonium, Mandela gave the panicky driver directions to Dullah Omar's house, and greatly surprised the Omar family by stopping in for a cold drink and a few minutes of peace and quiet. The house phone rang and it was an agitated Archbishop Tutu on the line, telling them to head for the Grand Parade, where the people were getting restless. 'If you do not return straight away, I cannot vouch for what will happen. I think there might be an uprising!'

Indeed, some of the people who had been waiting all day were starting to get unruly. Isolated incidents of looting were reported. Police fired shots. No one really knew what was going on. Journalists waiting for Mandela report that they relied for updates on people who were watching television in the nearby buildings.

Mandela's convoy finally arrived at the Grand Parade. At 8 pm, he appeared on the balcony of the City Hall to address the sea of people gathered below, their flags and banners held high. The very sight of him set them roaring and cheering.

'Amandla,' he called.

'Ngawethu,' they responded.

'iAfrica.'

'Mayibuye.'

He waited, and when the crowd finally calmed, he took out his speech and reached into his pocket for his glasses. Only to discover he had left them at Victor Verster. Wearing Winnie's glasses, he began to read in that distinctive voice that is so familiar to us now but which the assembled masses – and many millions of television viewers world-wide – were hearing for the very first time: 'Comrades and fellow South Africans, I greet you all in the name of peace, democracy and freedom for all. I stand here before you not as a prophet, but as a humble servant of you the people. Your tireless and heroic sacrifices have made it possible for me to be here today. I therefore place the remaining years of my life in your hands.'

He expressed gratitude – to the people of South Africa and all over the world who had campaigned for his release, and to his wife and family, whose pain and suffering, he said, was far greater than his own. He reiterated his loyalty to the ANC, and to the armed struggle. He expressed his hope that a negotiated settlement could soon be achieved, and that the armed struggle would no longer be needed.

The struggle was not over. It was beginning in a new form. He urged the crowd to intensify the struggle and 'we would walk the last mile together'. And he left them with this instruction: 'I hope you will disperse with discipline. And not a single one of you should do anything which will make other people to say that we can't control our own people.'

Valli Moosa, who had been part of the Nelson Mandela Reception Committee, and then part of the Internal Leadership Core of the ANC, worked closely with Mandela in the days leading up to his release. He recalled Mandela's thinking around the speech: 'He said they had put him in jail and now they are releasing him, but he does not want the people to get the impression that the years in prison had changed his beliefs. He was very clear that he was not going to show any sign of being a "reformed" man. He would say exactly what he would have said the day before he went into prison. The armed struggle continued, the conditions that made it necessary had not changed.'

MAKING FRIENDS
AND WINNING SUPPORT

From the very first days of freedom, Nelson Mandela displayed both a remarkable lack of bitterness at his incarceration, and a remarkable ability to work a room. He charmed, cajoled and co-opted all manner of people to his cause. And often left with a cheque.

Mandela called a press conference the day after his release from prison. He looked healthy, relaxed and cheerful. He greeted the South African journalists whose names he knew from their bylines, and thanked the press for keeping alive the stories of the imprisoned leaders. He went on to express his lack of bitterness. British journalist John Carlin, who was there, described it as 'an exercise in seduction from start to finish'.

Carlin wrote: 'He would now take charge openly, for all to see. Dashing all doubts, his first press conference as a free man was a tour de force, a master class in political persuasion.' The press conference ended on an extraordinary note, the likes of which Carlin hadn't seen in decades of reporting on politicians – 200 international journalists burst into 'spontaneous, heartfelt applause'.

Former British ambassador Robin Renwick recalls taking the newly released Mandela to Linger Longer, one of Johannesburg's poshest restaurants. It was a spot that attracted rich business types, and Renwick was a little concerned about his choice of venue. Unnecessarily, as it turned out. Mandela toured the room, introducing himself to his fellow diners, shaking hands, dashing into the kitchen to greet the staff. 'It was a bravura performance,' Renwick wrote.

WHO ARE YOU?

Just a week or two after his release from prison, Nelson Mandela was issued with his first South African passport. It wasn't his first passport, though. Mandela had previously had an Ethiopian passport, issued in 1962, giving his name as David Motsamayi (the name he used at Liliesleaf Farm, where he hid out on the pretext of being a labourer).

That year, when he was underground, Mandela left the country, without South African travel documents, via Lobatse in then Bechuanaland (now Botswana), travelling to a number of African countries to drum up political and economic support for the newly founded Umkhonto we Sizwe (MK).

His second passport wasn't entirely in the right name either, apparently – 'Rolihlahla' was spelt incorrectly as 'Rolilahla'.

Nonetheless, he traveled to Lusaka to meet the ANC's national executive committee. Within weeks of his release, Mandela set off to rally international support – starting in Africa. His trips were very strategic. Valli Moosa reminds us that he had a lot of time to think about what he wanted to say, what he would do, how he would conduct himself: 'His first trip was to Harare, not to London. In Tanzania, when he went to visit the MK camps, he put on his MK uniform. He'd thought a great deal about the kind of leadership needed in order for the ANC to be able to do what it needed to do in the coming years, which was to achieve a negotiated settlement that would be broadly supported not only in the ANC, but in society as well.'

MANDELA AND TAMBO, TOGETHER AGAIN

Nelson Mandela was out of prison, but South Africa was far from free. He was on a mission to foreign countries to

129

convince them to keep up the pressure on the South African government to speed up political change.

The first country he visited outside Africa was Sweden. The country had been a long-standing ally, at the forefront of global support for liberation. It was a good opportunity for Mandela to thank the Swedish people, but there was another, pressing reason for his visit – he was going to see the ANC president and his old friend and law partner, Oliver Tambo, who was in Sweden recuperating from a stroke, which had left him partially paralysed.

The two had last seen each other in Tanzania in 1962. They had communicated through secret channels while Mandela was incarcerated. Now they were to meet at a castle on a lake near Stockholm, to fill each other in and discuss the future of their now-legal organisation.

Valli Moosa recalled the warmth and joy with which the two men greeted each other, the ease with which they interacted after 28 years: 'They were both strong and powerful figures. Tambo was President of the ANC, the great leader of the revolution. Mandela was this great global figure. There could have been a bit of tension about who was in charge, but there was no such thing. It was wonderful.'

Mandela took to the position of deputy president of the ANC with ease. Moosa believes that the maturity of the relationship played a key role in ensuring the stability of the unbanned ANC. 'The various streams – MK, exile, internal – had very different cultures, different ways of doing things.

The two men, Oliver Tambo and Nelson Mandela, played a big role in holding them together.'

Mandela, travelling with Winnie, Moosa and a few others, was accorded a statesman's welcome. Swedish government officials and anti-apartheid campaigners, as well as South African exiles, gave them a warm and enthusiastic welcome. At a large public meeting Mandela thanked the Swedish people and pointed out that the ANC's ideological outlook was close to that of Sweden in many ways. Both shared a commitment to a progressive, enlightened society, to the upholding of human rights and democracy, and to striving towards egalitarianism.

Later that year, Oliver Tambo returned to South Africa to a tumultuous welcome. Nelson Mandela told the crowd who had turned out to greet the ANC president at Johannesburg's Jan Smuts Airport: 'We welcome him with open arms as one of the greatest heroes of Africa.'

MANDELA, PEACEMAKER

Mandela had precious little time to savour his freedom. He walked out of jail into a country aflame. In Natal, escalating political violence had turned the province into a war zone.

Just weeks after his release, as part of a desperately needed peace initiative, Mandela travelled to Durban to address a crowd of 100000: 'Friends, comrades, and the people of Natal, I greet you all. I do so in the name of peace, the peace that is so desperately and urgently needed in this region . . . My message to those of you involved in this battle of brother against brother is this: take your guns, your knives, and your pangas, and throw them into the sea. Close down the death factories. End this war now!'

It was a bold move – and a brave one, in front of a stirred-up and militant crowd. Journalist Allister Sparks, who was covering the rally, described how an angry hiss ran through the crowd, and his supporters listened sullenly to the rest of the speech. Perhaps for the first time, there was a less than positive response from Mandela's followers. Peace in Natal was beyond even Madiba. Instead, the next four years, leading up to the first democratic election in 1994, saw a significant escalation in violence. Some 14000 South Africans are believed to have died in politically related incidents during that time, with Natal a particular hotspot.

FREE MANDELA
(FROM MRS THATCHER!)

In July 1990, Mandela met British prime minister Margaret Thatcher at 10 Downing Street for the first time. It was hardly a match made in heaven. The two leaders had, historically, many areas of disagreement. Thatcher had opposed sanctions and distrusted the ANC for its strong communist contingent and talk of nationalisation. Nonetheless, she had pushed for Mandela's release, and was supportive of the negotiated settlement in South Africa.

When the meeting was first suggested, Mandela chatted to Robin Renwick, then British ambassador to South Africa, about how best to win over the Iron Lady. Renwick suggested a role play, with himself as Maggie, and Mandela as, well, himself. This appealed to Mandela's sense of humour, and he launched into telling 'Thatcher' about his fight for human rights. In turn, Renwick-as-Iron-Lady told him to 'stop all that nonsense about nationalising the banks and the mines'. Mandela responded that he'd learned it from the Brits!

Next, Renwick headed to London to brief Thatcher. He pointed out to her, presumably as diplomatically as one can, that Mandela had waited 27 years to tell his side of the story. Renwick wrote in his memoir, *Mission to South Africa*: 'She glared at me and said, "You mean I mustn't interrupt."'

When the two finally sat down together, Thatcher did as she'd promised, letting Mandela tell his story without interruption. He outlined the history of the ANC, and explained the current scenario. When it was her turn, she told him to 'stop talking about nationalising the banks and the mines' – just as Renwick had in their role play – which caused Mandela to burst out laughing.

The meeting stretched on for three hours, long past its expected end time, as the two discussed the new constitution, economics and other areas of mutual concern. The meeting went on so long that the bored – and notoriously iconoclastic – British journalists who were waiting outside in Downing Street took to chanting the familiar slogan, 'Free Nelson Mandela!'

THE MURDER OF CHRIS HANI

South African Communist Party leader Chris Hani pulled into the driveway of his Boksburg home, followed closely by a red Ford. From the car stepped a white man with a gun. He followed Hani to his front door and fired four shots at point-blank range, killing him instantly. The shots alerted Hani's 15-year-old daughter, Nomakhwezi, who opened the door to the sight of her father's body. Her screams drew the attention of a neighbour who arrived in time to see the shooter drive away.

Hani was the chief of staff of MK. He was widely beloved and respected – a survey found him the most popular political leader after Mandela – with a particular following among the youth. He was a revolutionary turned peacemaker, and his death was devastating – and potentially disastrous for peace and reconciliation.

The *Sunday Times* reported that ANC members gathered and formed a column on either side of the police mortuary van and broke into an emotional rendition of the farewell song for fallen comrades, 'Hamba Kahle M'konto'. Leaders came to the house – ANC National Chairman Oliver Tambo and his wife Adelaide, and son Dali; Mandela's lawyer Ismail Ayob, Walter Sisulu, Winnie Mandela . . . Tokyo Sexwale, then chairperson of the ANC's Gauteng region, wept.

As the news of Hani's murder spread, the crowd swelled. Emotions were running high. ANC leaders appealed for calm.

That day, 10 April 1993, was perhaps the most perilous single moment on the road to democracy. Anger was mounting and the country was on the brink of disaster.

It was Nelson Mandela who averted what could have been an uncontrollable eruption of rage at this assassination. In a television broadcast that night, he addressed the nation in his capacity as ANC president: 'Tonight I am reaching out to every single South African, black and white, from the very depths of my being . . .'

He spoke of the white foreigner who had killed Chris Hani and of the white Afrikaner woman who took down the assassin's number plate and reported it to the police.

'Now is the time for all South Africans to stand together against those who, from any quarter, wish to destroy what Chris Hani gave his life for – the freedom of all of us . . . Our decisions and actions will determine whether we use our pain, our grief and our outrage to move forward to what is the only lasting solution for our country – an elected government of the people, by the people and for the people.'

Even President De Klerk knew that only Mandela could save the country from disaster. As Mandla Langa, co-author of Mandela's memoir, *Dare Not Linger: The Presidential Years*, put it: 'When Chris Hani was killed, the seizing of that moment was when Mandela really became the de facto leader of the country.'

IN THE RING WITH ALI

Dear Mr Mandela
Allow me to extend to you and the A.N.C. my deepest regrets upon hearing of the death of Chris Hani. My prayers go out to Mr Hani's family and the people of South Africa during these difficult days.

I am providing you the following information regarding my itinerary should you desire to contact me (prior to our scheduled meeting on 19 April 1993):

CAPE SUN – 13 TO 16 APRIL – TEL: 021 238844
FAX: 021 238875
JOHANNESBURG GARDEN COURT – 16 TO 22
APRIL – TEL: 011 297011 FAX: 011 291515

Inshallah, I pray that God keeps you safe
Muhammed Ali

This signed letter from boxing great Muhammad Ali to Nelson Mandela offering his condolences on the death of Chris Hani was sold at auction in England for £7 200 in 2016. It was not, however, the letter that Mandela, in fact, received. Here's the story:

It so happened that Ali arrived in South Africa on 10 April 1993 – the very day that Chris Hani was assassinated outside his home in Boksburg. The personal assistant to the general manager of the Elangeni Hotel, in Durban, where Ali was staying at the time, typed up the letter of condolence, and made an error: 'Due to my nervous excitement about typing a letter of such historical importance I misspelt the name Muhammad replacing the last "a" with an "e". The letter was taken to Muhammad Ali and duly signed before someone noticed the error and returned it to me. I typed it again but kept the incorrect copy for posterity.' This is the letter that was auctioned.

In the wake of Hani's death, the country was on a knife edge. Grief and anger combined to create an unpredictable and volatile atmosphere. In spite of the danger, Ali attended Hani's funeral at the FNB Stadium. The crowd greeted him with chants of 'Ali! Ali!'. Not unlike Mandela, Ali was a great favourite of the people, and crowds greeted him wherever he went. On a visit to KwaMashu, outside Durban, crowds lined the streets as Ali's motorcade came through, with the boxer jogging alongside. Reports from the time say that they followed him into the local mosque chanting 'Ali the

Greatest', to which he raised his hand and replied, 'God is the Greatest.'

A famous series of photographs shows Nelson Mandela squaring up with Muhammad Ali. They met on a number of occasions over the years, and there was a genuine affection between the two men. While outwardly so different, they had much common ground, even beyond their shared love of boxing. Ali was outspoken on many of the same issues that Mandela cared so deeply about – in particular racism and inequality – and he felt a deep connection to Africa.

Both fought and sacrificed for their principles. Ali paid dearly for his refusal to serve in the US military during the Vietnam War. He was stripped of his heavyweight titles, sentenced to five years in prison, fined $10 000 and banned from boxing for three years.

Mandela was a big fan of the boxing champ – he even kept a picture of Ali on his desk. Writing in *The Independent*, Mandela described Muhammad Ali as 'not just my hero, but the hero of millions of young, black South Africans'. He wrote: 'He emerged as a hero in the USA at a time when black people were especially oppressed in that country. He emerged as a national hero and not as a hero of a black minority only . . . I thank Muhammad Ali for his strength of character and strength of purpose. I thank him for the courage he gave to me.'

The feeling was mutual. Ali was a huge admirer of Mandela, referring to him as a 'fellow freedom fighter, both in and out of the ring'. As soon as Mandela was released from prison, Ali expressed his eagerness to meet him. Which he did, on a number of occasions.

When Mandela died, Ali spoke of him as 'a man whose heart, soul and spirit could not be contained or restrained by racial and economic injustices, metal bars or the burden of hate and revenge. He taught us forgiveness on a grand scale . . . He inspired others to reach for what appeared to be impossible and moved them to break through the barriers that held them hostage mentally, physically, socially and economically. He made us realise, we are our brother's keeper and that our brothers come in all colours.'

DON'T MESS WITH MANDELA

As a politician, Mandela could be steely, although he was seldom outwardly angry. One exception occurred during the opening of the Convention for a Democratic South Africa (Codesa), the negotiating forum that was set up in December 1991 after the National Peace Accord was signed by the government, homeland governments and political organisations.

On the opening day, FW de Klerk asked to speak last. In his speech, he criticised the ANC, saying that 'an organisation which remains committed to the armed struggle cannot be completely trusted when it commits itself to peaceful negotiations'.

When De Klerk was finished, Mandela asked for special permission to speak, and when he did, he was furious and scathing: 'I am gravely concerned about the behaviour of Mr De Klerk today. He has launched an attack on the African National Congress, and in doing so he has been less than frank. Even the head of an illegitimate, discredited, minority regime as his, has certain moral standards to uphold. He has no excuse, because he is a representative of a discredited regime, not to uphold moral standards.'

Recalling that Codesa contretemps, journalist Sahm Venter told Danny Schechter, in *Madiba A to Z: The Many Faces of Nelson Mandela*, 'That was classic Madiba. No prepared speech. He just got back up on that stage and he let him have it, you know. Cutting him off at the knees. He could do that. I think he stands with a great deal of moral authority.'

He had sent a message to his opponents and to his followers – the time had come for negotiations, and Mandela was not going to be messed with.

This was not the first time the two men came into conflict and it was not to be the last. The tense relationship continued, and reached a new low over a domestic issue – who should live where. When Mandela was elected president in 1994, under the Interim Constitution, De Klerk became one of the two deputy presidents. De Klerk was told that he and his wife, Marike, could stay on in Libertas (now

Mahlamba Ndlopfu), the president's official residence in Pretoria, and Mandela would move into a residence called the Presidency. But the ANC wanted Mandela to move to Libertas, and to put the De Klerks in the Presidency. It all changed again, and the De Klerks were given Overvaal, formerly the home of the Transvaal provincial administrator. In his autobiography, De Klerk wrote that his wife was 'distressed by all the chopping and changing', which she saw as a deliberate humiliation.

Mandela and De Klerk had a fraught and often fractious relationship. You wouldn't know it to look at the famous picture of the two men at Nelson Mandela's inauguration as South Africa's new president, when he seized FW de Klerk by the hand and raised their palms in a joint display of triumph.

A SURPRISE VISIT FROM THE PRESIDENT

Debora Patta, Africa correspondent for CBS, was a young reporter on Radio 702 when she got the job of a lifetime – covering Nelson Mandela in the run-up to the first democratic election. For two years, she followed him around the country.

She remembers him as kind and solicitous. 'I was always

laden down with heavy radio equipment and a giant old Nokia cellphone, and he would offer to help me carry. Most of all he was very concerned that I was never going to find a boyfriend because I was always on the road with him. Then I started seeing someone, and in front of the other journalists he would ask how the relationship was going, which was quite mortifying. When I answered, "I'm actually getting married soon," he said, "Oh, I'll come to the wedding."

'I didn't think he meant it. You don't expect Nelson Mandela to come to your wedding. On the morning of the wedding the bodyguard phoned and said they needed to come and sweep the venue.

'He came with an entourage, and then word got out that he was there so other people just turned up to see him. There wasn't enough food. My Italian relatives were falling to their knees and kissing his ring as if he was the Pope. It was hilarious. Mandela is in all our wedding photos – there's him in his gold shirt and my sister in her bridesmaid's dress.'

Seeing him up close for those years, she was stuck by his genuine ability to be the same person, regardless of the circumstances. 'He was a wily man and a good strategist, but you never felt he was putting on a show. He genuinely did like kids, he wasn't just there for the photo op. He behaved in the same way, regardless. Mandela wasn't a saint, he was a real, flawed person, but he had a capacity for kindness. One time we were on the highway driving back from

Pretoria and we saw a woman stopped on the side of the road with a flat tyre. He tells the bodyguards to stop, which of course they don't want to do, stop on the highway in the dark with Mandela in the car, but he insists. Then he gets out and says to her, "Can I help you?" And all these strapping young men get out and change her tyre.'

One of her favourite memories is of accompanying him to Qunu: 'I remember us striding over the hills, this big tall man, and of course people coming out to see him. He loved it there, he was so excited, like a little kid, calling me over to show me, this is where we played this game, this is where I herded the goats. He had this beautiful sense of appreciation. He never spoke of what he'd missed out on, the losses, but I felt it there, a yearning.'

She got to see time and again his extraordinary effect on people: 'He was like a combination of a pop star and a Victorian gentleman. He had incredible natural charisma. People would go mad for him, even the people who thought they didn't like him. In the beginning, he had huge emotional and political significance for the ANC, but for many white South Africans, he was a terrorist. But he had this kind of charm, to men and women, which was how he managed to win over someone like Constand Viljoen.'

DISARMING HUMOUR

Things got very tense during multiparty negotiations in the run-up to the 1994 democratic election, but Mandela could also disarm people with his humour. He would occasionally tease the leader of the right-wing Freedom Front party, General Constand Viljoen, by saying, with a grin, 'We have to let the white man talk; after all, he is from the supreme race.' Awkward laughter would replace the charged atmosphere.

When Mandela referred to the opposition Democratic Alliance (DA) as a Mickey Mouse party, DA leader Tony Leon responded to the jibe saying that Mandela led a Goofy government. Years later, while in hospital awaiting surgery, Leon heard a knock on the door, followed by Mandela's distinctive voice saying, 'Hello Mickey Mouse, this is Goofy.'

He would often use self-deprecating humour to put other people at ease. When his presidential term was up, he would joke about being unemployed, or about his age.

THE NATIVE WHO CAUSED
ALL THE TROUBLE

In New Brighton township in the early 1960s, John Kani was one of the lookout boys who would keep an eye out when political meetings were under way. 'There was a blue van, I still remember the number plate, that belonged to the Special Branch. When we saw it we would whistle to show that the police were in the neighbourhood. One day we heard there was a very important person coming to a meeting organised by Raymond Mhlaba – I only found out later it was Nelson.'

John Kani first met Nelson Mandela in 1990, soon after Mandela's release. The acclaimed actor, director and writer recalled: 'People began to visit him at home – first the politicians, the religious people, the business people. At some stage, it was the turn of the cultural activists. About eight of us go to the house. He's sitting there on the chair, Winnie standing next to him and someone is introducing us, "Tata, this is so and so, Tata this is so and so," and when he comes to me Mandela says, "Ah, I know this one, he's the native who caused all the trouble . . ." That's what he called me until he died.'

The Native Who Caused All the Trouble is the name of a

play, written by Danny Keogh, Vanessa Cooke and Fink Haysom, in which Kani played a black man who refused to be evicted from a coloured area, because the land is God's, not man's, and 'cannot be exchanged like a shoe'. When Mandela was moved to Pollsmoor he watched a video of the play.

Mandela had heard of Kani's activism. He later told Kani that there was a tradition on Robben Island – when there was an incident in the place you came from, you would boast about it. Telling the story, Kani echoes Madiba: 'Like when you and Athol [Fugard] and Winston [Ntshona] got into trouble, I'd say to Walter, "You see, the boys are working in my province."'

Kani's contribution came in the form of his provocative plays, which became known as 'struggle theatre'. One of these was *The Island*, first produced in 1973.

Back when Kani was starting out with the Serpent Players, they put on the Greek tragedy *Antigone*. 'Shark, who played Haemon, never knew his lines. You didn't prompt Shark one word, you had to give the whole sentence. Our very first performance, Shark didn't come. So I stepped in. We found he'd been arrested, and he ended up on Robben Island for seven years. My uncle Harry was already on Robben Island doing five years. In a letter, he told me Shark was entertaining the prisoners at the quarry doing a one-man performance of *Antigone*. We couldn't believe it! He didn't know the lines! Apparently, he made it up.'

This and other stories from inmates blossomed into *The Island,* a play that brought John Kani, Winston Ntshona and Athol Fugard local and international acclaim (and Tony Awards). It also brought both Kani and Ntshona a stint in prison, detained without trial.

Two decades later, Kani got a call, and that famous voice came on the line: 'John, can you and Winston do that play, *The Island . . .*'

'I phoned Winston, we found a three-week gap, and we did it. That day, the theatre was filled with people from Shell House. Everyone was there. All the stalwarts and the comrades. UDF, trade unions, exiles. And Madiba in row F. There's a seat there with no seat in front of it, we always used that seat for him because of his long legs.

'As the lights went down I said, "Oh Winston, do you think he's going to like it? Do you think he's going to hate it?"'

There was a standing ovation.

'We went to meet him afterwards, and he just said: "Thank you." Ahmed Kathrada was with him, and he declared me and Winston honorary inmates of Robben Island. For me it was an honour much higher than the Tony Award.'

CHARMING THE JOURNOS

Journalist Rich Mkhondo was on 'Mandela lookout' for Reuters for a long while before the release, and was one of the first to interview him when he was free. Having covered Mandela at home and around the world, Rich has plenty of Madiba stories to share, although he says, 'I'm not sure how original some of them are – I think he did those kinds of things to everyone.'

When Mandela was in Texas to see George W Bush, Rich was there. 'Mandela pointed to me and said to Bush, "You see that guy there? He's a friend of mine, and he's been stalking me around the country. When the time comes for questions, I want you to let him go first." Then, when we went to Canada, he said the same thing to the Canadian Prime Minister!

'I gave him a copy of a book I wrote and weeks later I was at a press conference and in front of everyone he said "Rich, I wanted you to know I'm reading your book, I'm on page so and so . . ." He had a way of making people feel special. Not just me, everybody. I think it was a kind of banter, but it was more than that.

'Madiba invested in people who were going to help him relay his message. He knew the importance of journalists.

He knew that, during his incarceration, his story was kept alive by journalists. And he knew they were important to what he did now, so he made them feel special. He was firm but friendly, in a professional way. He would never say journalists shouldn't write anything bad about the ANC or the government.'

Anyone who had even a glancing association with Mandela felt that they had a personal connection, even if just in the moment. 'He was very clever, and remembered everything. It was remarkable the way he remembered names. I introduced him to my wife at his book launch, and when I saw him weeks later he asked after her by name.'

He had a number of endearing little tricks. 'At a function, he would introduce himself to everyone, "Hi, I'm Nelson Mandela . . ." As if anyone in the world would not know who he was. I asked once, and he said he didn't want to take for granted that everyone knows him.'

For journalists who covered Mandela, at the time, the moment they waited for was when he went off-script: 'We knew that the speech that he was reading was not important. The message didn't come from his heart. Once he started speaking off the cuff, that's when you got the real meat. The time he lambasted De Klerk at Codesa, that was a classic, but he did it many times. Read the speech that they'd written for him, and then he'd go off.'

⊚╱⊚

CONFLICT ABOUT
THE NOBEL PEACE PRIZE

In October 1993, Nelson Mandela and President FW de Klerk were jointly awarded the Nobel Peace Prize, following their compatriots Chief Albert Luthuli (in 1960) and Archbishop Desmond Tutu (in 1984).

Announcing the award in Oslo, the Nobel Committee said that De Klerk and Mandela had displayed 'personal integrity and great political courage' in finding a way forward to democracy, and had provided an example of peace and reconciliation.

George Bizos recalled that Mandela was not sure whether to accept the award jointly with the man who had spent most of his political life upholding apartheid, and whom he believed was allowing the continued killing of activists and civilians back home. In the end, he decided to go ahead and accept the award despite his misgivings.

Nadine Gordimer, the 1991 Nobel literature laureate, described it as 'a kind of betrayal' to see him share the prize with the apartheid president. Winnie Mandela later called it 'an insult' and 'a bribe, a gigantic plot to make him an instrument of peace for the white man'. Tokyo Sexwale later told the AFP news agency that there were those who thought

Mandela should decline the prize, and that it was Mandela who convinced them that he should go ahead and set an example of reconciliation.

The two men seemed to be pulling off a political miracle – the transformation of their country into a multiracial democracy – but relations between them were strained, and it showed. Even the photographs of that time show them as rather grim for two laureates.

In his acceptance speech, Mandela saluted his 'compatriot and fellow laureate', who 'had the courage to admit that a terrible wrong had been done to our country and people through the imposition of the system of apartheid'. He expected De Klerk to acknowledge the suffering that apartheid had caused, and its immorality, in his acceptance speech, but instead he maintained that 'both sides had made mistakes'.

When the two prizewinners appeared on the balcony of the Grand Hotel in Oslo, it was clearly Mandela the crowd were there to see. That De Klerk and Marike chatted during the singing of 'Nkosi Sikelel' iAfrika' did not go unnoticed.

George Bizos described how Mandela told his team not to write a speech for the private dinner with the Norwegian prime minister and 150 guests. There would be no press, so he'd just speak off the cuff: 'Nelson's patience finally snapped . . . In horrible detail he described the treatment of political prisoners on Robben Island, recounting an incident in which prison warders buried a man in the sand and urinated on him . . . "What mistakes did we make when you were brutalising us and locking us up and banning us and not allowing us to vote?" he asked angrily of De Klerk. This was the one and only occasion that I would ever see Nelson lose control and allow his personal feelings to spill out in public.'

At breakfast the next day, the two South African delegations sat separately from each other. De Klerk and his people left early, without saying goodbye to Mandela and his.

MANDELA
AS
PRESIDENT

MANDELA CASTS HIS VOTE

On 27 April 1994, 20 million people voted in South Africa's first democratic election. Very many of them voted for the first time. Among them was Nelson Mandela.

He wrote poignantly about that first vote in *Long Walk to Freedom*: 'I voted at Ohlange High School in Inanda, a green and hilly township just north of Durban, for it was there that John Dube, the first president of the ANC, was buried. This African patriot had helped found the organisation in 1912, and casting my vote near his grave site brought history full circle, for the mission he began eighty-two years before was about to be achieved.

'As I stood over his grave, on a rise above the small school below, I thought not of the present but of the past. When I walked to the voting station, my mind dwelt on the heroes who had fallen so that I might be where I was that day, the men and women who had made the ultimate sacrifice for a cause that was now finally succeeding. I thought of Oliver Tambo, and Chris Hani, and Chief Luthuli, and Bram Fischer. I thought of our great African heroes, who had sacrificed so that millions of South Africans could be voting on that very day; I thought of Josiah Gumede, GM

155

Naicker, Dr Abdullah Abdurahman, Lilian Ngoyi, Helen Joseph, Yusuf Dadoo, Moses Kotane. I did not go into that voting station alone on April 27; I was casting my vote with all of them . . . I marked an X in the box next to the letters ANC and then slipped my folded ballot paper into a simple wooden box; I had cast the first vote of my life.'

The decision to vote in Natal was partly strategic, too. For voters in the province, which had been wracked by violence and bloodshed in the run-up to the election, Mandela's presence showed that there was no danger in going to the polling stations.

It wasn't at all clear that this election would, in fact, go ahead peacefully and successfully. The IFP had decided at the last minute to participate. Most of the estimated 21.7 million eligible voters had never voted before, and many had no identity document, so the logistics were huge and complicated.

When the big day dawned, South Africans waited patiently for hours in long queues to claim their democratic right to vote. Many had waited decades to cast their first vote, what were a few more hours spent in a great snaking line of fellow citizens, waiting, too, for their chance to participate as full citizens of the country of their birth?

Yes, there were problems – misplaced ballots, rumours of voter fraud, logistical difficulties. But even these did not shake the determination of citizens to make this happen, peacefully.

And the mood! Well, you had to be there. South Africans

who were still speak of the camaraderie and celebration. The optimism. Many voters tell tales of meaningful moments of connection. Of generosity and good-heartedness. The 1994 election was not just a vote for a political party – it was a vote for peace and democracy.

A NEW SOUTH AFRICA, A NEW PRESIDENT

It took several days for the results to be counted. When the numbers were finally in, the ANC had polled 62.6 per cent of the national vote, giving it 252 of 400 seats in the National Assembly, slightly short of the two-thirds' majority that would give the party the right to push through constitutional changes without the support of the other parties. As outlined in the Interim Constitution, a Government of National Unity (GNU) was formed, and the IFP, NP and ANC were represented in Cabinet in proportion to the number of seats won in the elections.

On 9 May 1994, Nelson Mandela was elected the first black South African president by the National Assembly, with FW de Klerk and Thabo Mbeki as deputy presidents.

In *The New York Times*, correspondent Bill Keller wrote: 'The power that had belonged to whites since they first settled on this cape 342 years ago passed today to a

Parliament as diverse as any in the world, a cast of proud survivors who began their work by electing Nelson Mandela to be the first black president of South Africa . . . His giddy followers whooped in unparliamentary delight.'

South Africa was admitted to the Organization of African Unity (OAU) and resumed its seat in the General Assembly of the United Nations (UN).

The new president, Nelson Mandela, addressed the people of Cape Town on the Grand Parade:

Today we are entering a new era for our country and its people. Today we celebrate not the victory of a party, but a victory for all the people of South Africa. Our country has arrived at a decision. Among all the parties that contested the elections, the overwhelming majority of South Africans have mandated the African National Congress to lead our country into the future. The South Africa we have struggled for, in which all our people, be they African, Coloured, Indian or White, regard themselves as citizens of one nation is at hand.

He outlined a broad plan for the country: to tackle poverty, create jobs, promote peace and reconciliation, encourage investors and create a legal framework that would assist in the reconstruction and development of the country:

We place our vision of a new constitutional order for South Africa on the table not as conquerors, prescribing to the conquered. We speak as fellow citizens to heal the wounds of the past with the intent of constructing a new order based on justice for all.

This is the challenge that faces all South Africans today, and it is one to which I am certain we will all rise.

On 20 May 1994, the Senate (later renamed the National Council of Provinces) met for the first time under the control of the ANC, following its victory in seven of the nine provinces. The opening session of the bicameral Parliament took place four days later. The Constitutional Assembly met and was tasked with finalising the text of the Constitution.

THE PRESIDENTIAL INAUGURATION, THE PARTY EVERYONE WANTED TO BE AT

For many, it felt as if the new South Africa started on 10 May 1994, with the swearing-in of Nelson Mandela, now 75 years old, as the first democratic president, in front of the Union Buildings, the seat of the executive, before 100 000 free citizens.

This was the party everyone wanted to be at. For days before, foreign dignitaries had been arriving in the country. From America came Vice President Al Gore, First Lady Hillary Rodham Clinton, the Reverend Jesse Jackson and General

Colin Powell. There was Palestinian leader Yasser Arafat, Cuban President Fidel Castro and Zimbabwean President Robert Mugabe. Prince Philip. United Nations secretary-general Dr Boutros Boutros-Ghali, and many, many more from all over the world.

Local dignitaries took their seats, too. MK freedom fighters brushed shoulders with generals of the old South African Defence Force. A rabbi, an imam and a priest followed each other onto the stage. The crowd on the lawn below watched their arrival on huge screens on either side of the stage. Particular favourites raised a cheer from a crowd that was swelling by the minute, festive and friendly, and appropriately Rainbow Nation. For many, this was perhaps the first time they'd been in such a convivial, multiracial group. Strangers hugged, chatted, danced, brought together by their mutual awe and joy. A group of young people ran across the lawn holding a coffin with 'hamba kahle apartheid' (farewell apartheid) painted on the side. Entrepreneurs sold T-shirts.

When the president-elect Nelson Mandela was announced, the response was a deafening cheer. Ukubonga (the traditional art form of praise singing) followed. Royal poet Zolani Mkiva gave a stirring performance. He translated his praise poem thus:

There, Mandela. There is Mandela. There is the son of the soil. He has no perfumed lips. He speaks the truth. He has no cat

eyes but he can see the true colours of the universe. He has
no dog nose but he can smell and distinguish between carbon
monoxide and oxygen. He has no donkey ears but he can hear
what makes sense and what is a nuisance. He is the son of the
soil, a brother to the daughters of the land.

The formalities continued. The national anthem – first 'Die
Stem', then 'Nkosi Sikelel' iAfrika' – as the new flag ran up
the pole and the crowd roared 'Amandla!'. When Mandela
swore allegiance to the new republic and its constitution,
and as the words 'So help me God' left his lips, the shout
came back: 'Viva Nelson Mandela, Viva.'

Archbishop Desmond Tutu led the prayer 'God Bless
Africa'. Mandela's speech was a triumph of inclusivity and
hope:

The time for the healing of the wounds has come.
The moment to bridge the chasms that divide us has come.
The time to build is upon us.

…

Let there be justice for all.
Let there be peace for all.
Let there be work, bread, water and salt for all.
Let each know that for each the body, the mind and the soul
have been freed to fulfil themselves.
Never, never and never again shall it be that this beautiful land
will again experience the oppression of one by another and

suffer the indignity of being the skunk of the world.
Let freedom reign.
The sun shall never set on so glorious a human achievement!
God bless Africa!
Thank you.

Then the cannons boomed out the presidential salute, and the military aircraft and helicopters flew overhead in formation, trailing the new South African flag, fluttering brightly against a crisp blue autumn sky, over the lawns packed with people. The crowd screamed its approval. This was their air force now.

THERE IS NO MORE YOU AND US

Everyone wanted to be part of the inauguration of Nelson Mandela as the first president of a democratic South Africa. But, of course, the grounds of the Union Buildings couldn't handle the immense numbers of people who wanted to be there.

In order for Joburgers to celebrate close to home, the proceedings at the Union Buildings would be televised and played on the big screen at Ellis Park Stadium, where a big soccer match between Bafana Bafana and Zambia was taking place. Mandela himself would make an appearance. It was a genius idea – 60 000 people were in the stadium instead of clogging up the roads to Pretoria.

Rory Steyn, commander of the police VIP Protection Unit in Johannesburg, was responsible for advance security, that is, making sure that the venue was 'secure and sterile' before the president arrived. He takes up the story:

'I went to Ellis Park to await the arrival of the newly inaugurated President. We brought the sniffer dogs through, and posted men and women at the entrances, the same as I would have done when the previous State President went to the rugby. I told myself, you now have a new President, which the majority of South Africans voted for, now go do your job.

'Having just sworn the oath of office, Nelson Mandela flew the 60 kilometres south to Johannesburg. He would then turn around and fly back to host the lunch for 184 heads of state. He was a bit late, because the proceedings ran late – it was not his fault, I learnt later that he was never late. The helicopter landed at the Technikon, and from there, a vehicle took him round the corner, up the vehicle ramp, and right up to the glass doors of the Presidential Suite. The South African Football Association officials welcomed the President and at halftime he went down to greet the teams, and then through the tunnel and onto the field to greet the crowd.

'He gets back in the car and is about to leave – there are 184 heads of state waiting for him for lunch – and I can see he's trying to get out of the vehicle. It's a 3.8 tonne armoured BMW; you don't just open that door, you need someone on the outside to give it a sharp tug. So he gets out and, without saying a word, heads towards an old-school South African Police colonel who is standing there in his full dress blues, stars and castles on his shoulders. As the President gets closer, this guy's eyes are getting bigger and bigger. He puts out his hand, and says, "Colonel, I just want you to know that today you have become our police. There is no more you and us." This old guy started crying, tears streaming down his face. Madiba pats him on the shoulder and gets back in the car.

'This is a powerful memory. I was a lieutenant colonel at the time and I can tell you, when Mandela came out of prison four years before, saying we were one country, everyone black and white, I didn't believe him. This cynical old cop thought, yeah, well, that's the official line, you're a politician, of course you're going to say that.

'What I saw was a very private, very personal exchange. There was no press there, no PR opportunity. No one watching. From that day, I started to question what I thought and what I'd been taught. I realised he was the one who can possibly unite South Africa, and he did. It was the day that changed my life.'

MONEY WHERE YOUR MOUTH IS

When he took office, one of Mandela's first acts was to reduce his R700 000 presidential salary. He and his deputy presidents took 20 per cent pay cuts, and the salaries of lower-ranking officials were cut by up to ten per cent.

He said this would set an example of the kind of fiscal discipline the country needed to address the social and economic ills it faced. The euphoria of the first democratic election and the new dispensation was dampened by the realisation that, far from being rich, robust and efficient, South Africa's economy was in dire straits and in desperate need of reconstruction. The effects of decades of apartheid were enormous – inequality in terms of income and wealth; overwhelmingly white ownership of land, businesses and other resources; a lack of service and infrastructure provision in black areas; and inefficient duplication of government services and departments.

Inflation was in double digits and the country had massive public debt. For the new government, tackling these issues necessitated public spending cuts at a time when they needed to spend on eradicating poverty, creating employment and funding the Reconstruction and Development Programme (RDP). In his first address to Parliament,

165

Mandela announced that government would, in the first 100 days, implement Presidential Lead Projects, programmes that would focus on major areas of desperate need. These prioritised free medical care for children under six and pregnant women, a feeding scheme in impoverished primary schools and the electrification of 350 000 homes.

IT'S ALL ABOUT THE CHILDREN

One chilly night, not long before he was elected president, Nelson Mandela took a late-night walk through the streets of Cape Town. As he stepped out, a group of street children approached him. His bodyguards tried to shoo them away, but Mandela said no, he wanted to talk to them. The children asked him a strange question, 'Why do you love us?'

Bongi Mkhabela, CEO of the Nelson Mandela Children's Fund, relates the story: 'He tossed and turned thinking about these children who felt so unloved that they were perplexed by the emotion. Unable to sleep, he resolved in his own heart that when he does become President he will establish a foundation that would change how our society treats children. The Children's Fund was really born in his heart.'

On the first celebration of Youth Day, 16 June 1994, he announced the establishment of the Nelson Mandela Children's Fund (NMCF) and pledged to pay a third of his own salary into it annually to get it started. He called on others to do the same. He was the most remarkably effective fund-raiser. Nobody could resist the Madiba magic. Corporations and individuals rallied to support the fund. Mkhabela smiles, 'Every CEO of the time will tell you when Mandela called for a breakfast, he also said, "Bring your chequebook." When people said they wanted to give him money, he would say, "Make the cheque out in the name of the Nelson Mandela Children's Fund."' Staff members from that time remember him returning from a trip or event and patting down his pockets for cheques to hand over.

He raised money from all over the world. Everyone wanted a piece of – and a pic with – Madiba. Celebrities flocked to meet the great man – Michael Jackson, the Black Eyed Peas, Denzel Washington, Annie Lennox, Elton John, Naomi Campbell, Beyoncé, Quincy Jones, Will Smith, Spike Lee and David Beckham, to name but a few. While the stars got their photo ops, Mandela would take the opportunity to call on them to support his charities, in particular the NMCF. Nelson Mandela was asking for help for South Africa's children who had suffered under apartheid. Who could turn him down?

Speaking at the official launch of the Fund in 1995, he opened with these words: 'There can be no keener revelation of a society's soul than the way in which it treats its children.'

The Fund initially operated as a grant-making organisation, promoting a humanitarian response to the plight of South Africa's children and youth. The 'handout' approach was unsustainable, and the Fund repositioned itself as a development organisation. A child is always seen in the context of family and community. Today, the NMCF focuses on child survival and development through the First 1 000 Days initiative; protection and safety, through the Safe Schools programme; and youth leadership.

At the Fund's Saxonwold offices, the stamp of Mandela is clear. There are pictures of him, photographs of him with the first board, with children. Most importantly, his spirit guides the organisation. Mkhabela says, 'We live by the values that he envisaged. He was very principled in everything he did. Inclusivity was very important, we are here for *all* children, throughout South Africa, all races, disabled children, and we also engage with mothers and grandmothers, and local leaders. We realised that we have to create an ecosystem that supports the child.'

She gives an example of how ethical he was in his leadership. He wanted the Fund to have a permanent home, its own building, but the board of trustees turned down the idea, saying that the money he had raised was for children, and couldn't be used for bricks and mortar. She recalls, 'He was chairman at the time and could have pushed it through, but he didn't. He subjected himself to the rule of people he had asked to help him with the foundation. He would honour and respect their decision. He asked if he could raise the money for the building, they agreed, and he went out and did it.'

COOKING FIT FOR A KING

Brett Ladds was a young chef when he got a break that would lead to him cooking for kings and queens and celebs – and Nelson Mandela.

Brett's mentor, chef Christian Michel, was asked by Minister of Foreign Affairs Pik Botha to come and take charge of the Presidential Guesthouse for the new ANC-led government. Soon-to-be President Mandela would be staying at the guest-house until his permanent residence was ready. It was a short-term gig, and Brett was to come with him.

He recalled: 'It was so busy. But a few weeks after the inauguration things settled down. I would cook supper for Madiba and then feed his bodyguards. Some nights he was out and if there were no cars or bodyguards around by 6 pm, I would lock up and go home. One night, early on, I was locking up. I thought I was alone and I was singing to myself while I walked down the long marble passage and I heard his voice: "Who's there?"

'I wanted to turn around and leave but I went into the room and there was President Mandela in a big green wing-back chair. I said, "It's you!" It was the first time he had talked to me and I was so scared, I was shivering. He asked why I was so scared and I blurted out, "Why haven't you killed us yet?" I still believed what the apartheid government had told us, I thought whites would be killed. He laughed and said: "If I must live for yesterday I'd rather die today than see tomorrow." He calmed me down, and thanked me for looking after him.'

Not long after that interaction, Ladds was asked if he would like to stay on. Mandela was living alone, and the chef was asked to move into a wing of the guesthouse.

'It was weird at first. At night I could sometimes hear him walking around and I'd go and ask if he needed anything, could I bring him some tea. One night I was cooking supper and my wife was trying to get the kids organised. Our youngest was a baby and Keagan was in preschool. He had to learn the colours of the rainbow for homework. It was chaos.

'There was a knock on the door and it was Mandela. He said: "Can I help?" My wife was trying to be casual but I knew she was having ten heart attacks. He came in and took over the homework while I cooked. He taught Keagan the colours of the rainbow, and Keagan said, "Thank you, Tata". It turned out the two of them had already met.

'My son got a gold star for his rainbow colours and he ran down to show Madiba, who was just going in to some state banquet. He stopped to speak to Keagan and congratulate him. It got into the newspapers.'

It's just one of many stories Ladds tells of Mandela's

warmth, his concern for others, including the staff. 'He was a great listener. In fact, he didn't speak a lot, but when he did you could hear a pin drop,' said Ladds.

'There were so many famous people in and out and they were all star-struck by Madiba, all of them. Even the Queen. And the Pope – I saw him come down and take Madiba's arm to help him on the stairs. They would treat him as a beloved elder.

'And the ordinary people too. A farmer would arrive at the gate and say, "I grew these mushrooms on my farm for the President."'

JUSTICE FOR ALL
AT THE CONSTITUTIONAL COURT

On 14 February 1995, 11 judges, clad in green robes, took their oaths of office in front of President Mandela and the Minister of Justice, Dullah Omar. South Africa's Constitutional Court was formally opened, with Chief Justice Arthur Chaskalson as president. It's hard to imagine the significance of that day in the country's history, and in its law.

South Africa's Constitutional Court was established in 1994, in terms of the Interim Constitution of 1993. It was a new court, to protect the Constitution and the fundamental human rights it entrenches. It is the country's highest legal authority in all constitutional matters and is the key institution of our constitutional democracy.

Speaking at the inauguration of the Constitutional Court in 1995, Nelson Mandela said the following:

The last time I appeared in court was to hear whether or not I was going to be sentenced to death. Fortunately for myself and my colleagues we were not. Today I rise not as an accused but, on behalf of the people of South Africa, to inaugurate a court South Africa has never had, a court on which hinges the future of our democracy.

It is not just a building that we inaugurate, handsome though it is. It is not a body of wise men and women that we launch on their path, important though we regard their work. It is not just our blessings that we give to their work, confident as we are in their integrity and commitment to justice. It is an institution that we establish – South Africa's first Constitutional Court.

People come and people go. Customs, fashions, and preferences change. Yet the web of fundamental rights and justice which a nation proclaims must not be broken. It is the task of this court to ensure that the values of freedom and equality which underlie our Interim Constitution – and which will surely be embodied in our final Constitution – are nurtured and protected so that they may endure.

Remember that up until 1994, the judiciary was overwhelmingly white and male. Given that, and the history of apartheid laws, there was a question around legitimacy, and how all communities could experience – and feel – a real sense of justice. Mandela's opening address continued with these words:

No office and no institution can be higher than the law. The highest and the most humble in the land all, without exception, owe allegiance to the same document, the same principles. It does not matter whether you are black or white, male or female, young or old; whether you speak Tswana or Afrikaans; whether you are rich or poor or ride in a smart new car or walk barefoot; whether you wear a uniform or are locked up in a cell. We all have certain basic rights, and those fundamental rights are set out in the Constitution.

The Constitutional Court needed a new home. The site that was chosen was the infamous Number Four, the Old Fort Prison in Braamfontein, Johannesburg. A site that is steeped in apartheid history and injustice, it has been transformed into the site of justice and equality. The building itself is beautiful, and filled with symbolism. The court building incorporates 150 000 bricks from the demolished awaiting-trial block of the former prison. It was designed on the theme of 'Justice under a tree', a traditional form of dispute resolution. Shafts of light enter the foyer as if through leaves in a forest. The tree is represented in the court's logo as well.

At the entrance, the words 'Constitutional Court' are

173

written in South Africa's 11 official languages. The doors to the court have the 27 rights of the Bill of Rights carved into them. A stairwell from the prison bears the Portuguese words, '*A luta continua*' (the struggle continues). The roof's concrete beams are inscribed with the words 'human dignity, equality and freedom' in samples of the handwriting of each of the judges incumbent during the building of the court.

On Human Rights Day, 21 March 2004, the Court's permanent home was inaugurated by President Thabo Mbeki, Mandela's successor. Twenty-seven children born in 1994, South Africa's first year of democracy, recited the Bill of Rights in the country's 11 official languages.

The Constitution Hill precinct and the Court itself form a popular attraction for tourists and for South Africans. Visitors are rewarded with insight and understanding of the complex and layered history of the place, enjoy its thoughtful architecture and its collection of over 200 artworks by artists such as Cecil Skotnes, Gerard Sekoto and William Kentridge.

If you visit, don't miss the 'We the People' wall, running the length of Constitution Square, which displays the opinions of visitors to Constitution Hill. One of the contributors is none other than the man who inaugurated the Constitutional Court, former president Nelson Mandela.

REUNION AT ROBBEN ISLAND

Visit Robben Island today and the tour takes you past the famous lime quarry where political prisoners broke rocks and shovelled the lime that was used for whitewashing houses and paving the island's roads.

Near the entrance to the quarry stands a cairn, or pile of rocks. Cairns have been made by humans since ancient times as memorials or landmarks. Your tour guide – they are all ex-political prisoners – will tell you the story of this particular pile of rocks . . .

On 11 February 1995, five years after Nelson Mandela's release, Robben Island hosted a reunion of 1 300 ex-political prisoners. It was an emotional experience, revisiting the place where they had been incarcerated and reconnecting with fellow prisoners, known and unknown.

Visiting the quarry must have been particularly painful for these men. It was here that prisoners undertook arduous labour under the blazing sun and in the chilly wind off the Atlantic Ocean. The glare reflected from the white rock damaged the eyes, and the quarry dust settled in the lungs. Many prisoners, including Mandela, developed eye and respiratory problems as a result.

At the same time, the lime quarry was the place where

Mandela and his colleagues learned and taught, discussed and strategised. It was the centre of 'The University'.

Returning to the quarry as a free man and president of a democratic South Africa, Mandela spontaneously placed a stone near the quarry entrance. Other ex-political prisoners followed suit. Soon there was a small pile of stones, each placed there by a man who had given some piece of his life to the creation of a free and democratic South Africa.

@ ⁄ ⊚

IT WAS THE TIME OF MY LIFE . . .

Vanessa Mitchell has been working on Robben Island since 1997. She was a tour guide when Nelson Mandela visited the island on 24 September 1997 to officially open the Robben Island Museum. Vanessa was given the task of fetching him from the helipad and driving him to the prison hall. She tells the story:

'I fetched him. Don't ask me who else was there, I don't remember anyone else but him and me. But we were on our way and they radioed me to say, "Just drive him around a bit, because the guests haven't arrived yet." So I drove him round and round. And he said, "Why are we driving round and round?" I explained why I had to do it, and he said, "No my dear, just get me to the prison hall."

'You know how he loved children. On his way in to open

the museum, he grabbed the baby of one of my colleagues, a child of about a year old, and walked in with the baby and did the ceremony like that.

'Then I had to take him back. He remembered my name, from when I introduced myself before the ceremony. Then he got out and walked away and then turned and said, "Are you not going to ask me to take a photo with you?" I had my camera in my pocket, but I didn't want to ask. I was being polite and he recognised that, and put me at ease.

'I was overwhelmed by him. It was an honour to fetch him to take him there, and for him to ask me if I wanted a photo. It was unheard of in someone of his stature.'

UNITED IN RUGBY

There's an iconic photograph that almost every South African recognises – Nelson Mandela, in green and gold jersey and cap, presenting the Webb Ellis Cup to Springbok captain Francois Pienaar. Mandela has his hand on the captain's shoulder, congratulating him, and Pienaar is beaming. It's an extraordinary moment – the newly democratic South Africa has won the 1995 Rugby World Cup.

Rugby was traditionally an almost entirely white sport, strongly associated with Afrikaners. It was emblematic of apartheid South Africa. International sporting sanctions dramatically reduced the opportunities for South African teams to play, and when they did, as a matter of principle, many South Africans would support the opposing side.

Yet, in 1995, South Africa was to host the world at the premier event on the international rugby calendar. What would the majority of South Africans relate to in a bunch of big white guys thundering into each other?

With his extraordinary mixture of political astuteness and human touch, Mandela turned what might have been an irrelevant or even divisive sporting event into a remarkable act of nation-building. He maintained that the Springboks were 'our' team, the 'Amabokoboko', representing the whole of the new South Africa.

The Springbok team learned the new national anthem, 'Nkosi Sikelel' iAfrika', which they sang before the final. Mandela wore the team shirt. The crowd – mostly the traditional demographic of white Afrikaners – chanted his name. And the team won 15–12 against the All Blacks in extra time, sending the nation into a frenzy of celebration.

MELKTERT IN ORANIA

In August 1995, struggle stalwart Amina Cachalia received an invitation to accompany her dear friend Nelson Mandela to visit an old woman in the Northern Cape.

Cachalia had her reservations about the visit. The old woman was Betsie Verwoerd, the spouse of former prime minister Hendrik Verwoerd, the 'architect of apartheid'. And the destination was Orania, a white enclave established by hardline Afrikaners on private land in the Karoo.

But she came round to the idea, as she wrote in her autobiography, *When Hope and History Rhyme*: 'I should indicate my scepticism that belonged to the yesteryears of my world . . . I realised that we were on the threshold of a new beginning. I was happy and proud to be at his side on this journey to Orania.'

After first visiting Veronica Sobukwe, the widow of Robert Sobukwe, in Alice in the Eastern Cape, Mandela, Cachalia and Albertina Sisulu flew to Orania where they were received in the community centre.

It is a picture that borders on the surreal – Nelson Mandela and Betsie Verwoerd chatting over tea and coffee, melktert and koeksisters, in the company of the Verwoerd daughter, Anna, and of course Cachalia and Sisulu. Verwoerd's son-in-law, Carel Boshoff, the founder of Orania, hovered about.

'I have looked forward to this with eagerness,' Mandela apparently told a smiling Betsie Verwoerd, 94, 'I am happy to be here.'

Verwoerd had once lived the life of a first lady, in beautiful official residences in Pretoria and Cape Town. Nelson Mandela had spent 27 years in prison as a result of her husband's policies. And now Mandela was living in her one-time home, and she was living in self-imposed exile in a dusty dorp in the middle of nowhere.

After tea, this odd group walked over to the monument to Verwoerd. Mandela posed next to it. As Cachalia tells the story, 'There on the top of a koppie was this tiny statue of the man who had ruled our lives with an iron fist. Madiba stood – a giant – looking down on this wee statue and quipped: "I didn't realise he was so small." I controlled a burst of laughter by looking around for a distraction.'

Mandela was devoted to the idea of reconciliation, and was a master of the grand symbolic gesture. The visit to Betsie Verwoerd was applauded by some as a generous gesture of racial reconciliation during a turbulent time. Others thought that Mandela had taken his reconciliation efforts too far. After all, it was Verwoerd who had taken the ideas of apartheid and created the laws that denied black people the right of citizenship, and condemned them to a hopeless education.

As they returned to the aircraft for the last leg of their trip – to visit Nokukhanya Luthuli, widow of Chief Albert Luthuli – Amina Cachalia gave a sigh of relief and said to Mandela: 'Never, ever bring me here again.' He threw back his head and laughed.

DANCING WITH THE QUEEN

Not many would dare to call Queen Elizabeth II anything but 'Your Majesty'. And nobody would dream of addressing her as 'Elizabeth'. Prince Philip, the Duke of Edinburgh, alone has that honour. Well, Prince Philip and Nelson Mandela. Madiba famously didn't stand on ceremony around the British monarch, whom he apparently rather admired. She seemed not to mind his familiarity – maybe it made a change from the usual formality.

During Mandela's state visit to the United Kingdom in 1996, instead of a traditional state dinner to return the Queen's hospitality – he stayed at Buckingham Palace as an honoured guest – he hosted an evening of music and dance to raise money for his Nations Trust to help schoolchildren back home. It was an all-star event – Tony Bennett, Quincy Jones, Phil Collins, Hugh Masekela and Benjamin Zephaniah were among the performers – held at the Royal Albert Hall (which Mandela apparently referred to as 'this big round building').

The highlight of the evening was South Africa's Ladysmith Black Mambazo. When they came on stage, Nelson Mandela, dressed in a black silk shirt, got to his feet for his customary Madiba dance – in the Royal Box! The Prince of Wales was swaying and clapping. The Duke of Edinburgh joined in, followed by the Queen who, in the words of the next morning's *Daily Telegraph*, 'has seldom been known to boogie in public'.

Nelson Mandela had got the Queen on the dance floor! As Robin Renwick, then British ambassador to South Africa, observed drily in his memoir of the time, 'This was not a feat that could have been accomplished by any other world leader.'

WOZA NELSON MANDELA, WELCOME PRINCE CHARLES

Mandela's visit to Brixton, London, was something between a royal visit and a carnival. More than 10 000 people – many with Madiba's face emblazoned on their T-shirts – jammed the streets. A banner on the Brixton Recreation Centre read: 'Woza Nelson Mandela, Welcome Prince Charles'.

Shops and houses and balconies were festooned with decorations and welcome signs. Reggae music pumped from sound systems, competing with choirs and the calls of Brixton hawkers selling videos of Mandela's release from prison. Boys and girls who had been kept home from school for the occasion shimmied up street poles to get a better view. Locals came out in their best African dress. When they finally caught a glimpse of their hero, some of the assembled fans burst into tears.

Mandela had insisted on putting Brixton on the list of places to visit on his whirlwind 1996 tour of London. The largely black neighbourhood had often been a hotbed of racial tension and had been the scene of rioting in 1981. Many Brixton residents had suffered prejudice and intolerance, and the area was a centre of anti-apartheid and anti-racist activity during the struggle years.

Mandela said at the time: 'The masses of the people in this country were in the forefront of our struggle. I am looking forward to going to Brixton to thank them for their help.' *The New York Times* commented: 'It was officially labeled a state visit, but . . . Nelson Mandela's four-day triumphal sweep through London looked more like a coronation.' When the 'king' of said coronation insisted on walking a bit, he was given a rapturous welcome from the crowd. Newspapers reported that security got uneasy when someone put a girl over the railings to give flowers to Mandela. Mandela and Prince Charles were bundled into the car, and headed for South Africa House in Trafalgar Square where Mandela was to give a speech.

The impassioned crowd gave chase. When the car was gone and the jubilant crowd had dispersed, a jumble of shoes was left, stretching the length of Brixton Road, abandoned by their owners in pursuit of their hero, Nelson Mandela.

REACH FOR A DREAM

Ahmed Kathrada tells a story that illustrates President Mandela's love of children, and his ability to make a grand gesture.

Kathrada was escorting Nadine Gordimer on a tour of Robben Island, when a young girl asked him to pose with her for a photograph. He learned that the child, Michelle Brits, had leukaemia, and that her visit to Robben Island had been arranged by the Reach for a Dream Foundation, in part-fulfilment of her dearest wish. The girl's other wish was to meet President Mandela.

When he returned home, Kathrada told Madiba the story, and asked if he could arrange for Michelle to visit him at his home or office. 'His response was pure and vintage Mandela,' wrote Kathrada.

'I don't think we should give this young girl the trouble of coming all the way to me. Let's rather go to her,' Mandela suggested.

And so the President, with his already jammed schedule, got on a plane and flew to Secunda, in Mpumalanga, to fulfil the dream of a gravely ill child. The whole town turned out to welcome him, and to pray for her recovery.

Kathrada describes the emotional meeting between this

young Afrikaans girl and the elderly black president: 'As she clasped her little arms around his neck and kissed him, the eyes of millions must have filled with tears just as mine did . . .'

'ASIMBONANGA' – WE HAVE NOT SEEN HIM . . .

There's a YouTube video of Johnny Clegg and Juluka at an international symposium on Africa in Germany, in 1997, that's been viewed over 6 million times. Clegg introduces the song 'Asimbonanga': 'In 1986, South Africa was in a State of Emergency and there was a very intense cultural struggle that was being waged. And we were part of that. This is a song we wrote for truly one of the greatest South Africans that ever lived, Nelson Mandela, and we'd like to open the show tonight with a tribute to him . . .'

The band takes up the song, which was written about Nelson Mandela's imprisonment on Robben Island:

Asimbonanga (we have not seen him)
Asimbonang' umandela thina (we have not seen Mandela)
Laph'ekhona (in the place where he is)
Laph'ehleli khona (in the place where he is kept)

Unknown to Clegg, as he sings the man himself appears on stage behind him, to the absolute joy of the crowd.

He describes it: 'We go into the chorus, and the crowd roars, about 1 500 people, and I think, "Wow, they know my song". With more gusto, I carry on and in the middle of the verse there's another kind of crowd acknowledgment and a wave, and I think, what's going on? I turn round and behind me Nelson Mandela is being led onstage by my backing vocalist, Mandisa Dlanga.'

As he tells the story 20 years later, Clegg shakes his head in disbelief at the memory: 'It was a moment that was completely psychologically destabilising. I had no idea that he was even at the conference. I finished the song, and went over to him and said, "Do you want to say something?" And he said that completely wonderful line, "It is music, and dancing that makes me at peace with the world. And at peace with myself."'

And then Mandela says, 'But I don't see much movement at the back there. Let's just repeat!' The band plays the chorus again, the crowd now on their feet, the elderly Madiba doing his distinctive shuffle. And then the two men leave the stage, arm in arm.

Clegg describes the extraordinary trajectory of that song, which was written in a time of great violence and repression. It was banned in South Africa, so it couldn't be played on the radio, but it became an underground hit in the townships.

'I was in a rundown house in Bertrams with my band, rehearsing, and we heard that two or three township youths had been shot dead by the army. I thought to myself, this is the emergence of a civil war, when the army shoots its own citizens. I was so depressed that when the guys went out to get lunch – Russian and chips and fresh white bread – I stayed and picked up my guitar.

'I wondered, how can I write about Nelson Mandela and his incarceration, not as a propagandist, but in a way that would make people think about it from a different angle. As artists in the apartheid era, we had huge debates about culture as a weapon. For me, art is not a weapon, the artist has to come to the subject with complete freedom and find their own angle, to find the particular in the universal, and the universal in the particular.

'I came up with the concept that the thing that linked everybody, whether you were right wing or left wing, Marxist, capitalist or racist, was that we did not know what he looked like. Asimbonanga, we haven't seen him.

'I used the concept of the island, but I went back to John Donne, "No man is an island". In the poem, he writes that every person who dies is like a clod of earth coming off the continent. As long as Mandela was on Robben Island, we were all islands, we couldn't be whole.

'When I wrote those words, I had no inkling that 11 years later I would be in another country, and the man I was sing-ing about would sing and dance with me. The moment

I turned around and saw him, all of those things came together. That moment is the pinnacle of my career as a songwriter, as someone who sat down and worked out lyrics, to tell a story that could make even conservative white people think a bit about how we can overcome this separation we have created. It was like the universe saying, "Good". And, unbelievably, they filmed it!'

TWO PRESIDENTS

Mandela's and Bill Clinton's presidential terms overlapped. The two leaders met on many occasions, from their first encounter at the Democratic Party National Convention in 1992 to 2012, when Bill and his daughter, Chelsea, visited Mandela at his home.

Journalist Rich Mkhondo tells of a White House reception Mandela attended with black religious and educational leaders at the height of the scandal over Clinton's affair with intern Monica Lewinsky.

At the function, Mandela abandoned his intention not to interfere in the scandal. 'We are aware of the national debate that is taking place in this country about the president, and it is not our business to interfere in this matter. But we do wish to say that President Clinton is a friend of South Africa and Africa. And I believe the friend of the great mass of black people, and the minorities and the disabled of the United States,' Mandela said to applause. 'We have often said that our morality does not allow us to desert our friends. And we will doubtless say tonight: we are thinking of you in this difficult and discouraging time in your life.'

Clinton said that Mandela would be very firm if his country had a position that disagreed with the American position. The two men might argue, but when they weren't arguing, they were friends. They would talk about life, kids, managing emotions. They spoke often on the phone, said Clinton: 'We used to do business together on the phone where the time difference was so great I would take the call at night. And if it wasn't too late Mandela would make me go get Chelsea every time he called and he would talk to her and ask her if she was doing her homework.'

HELLO, NEIGHBOUR

In the leafy Johannesburg suburb of Houghton, residents might be disturbed on a Saturday afternoon by a guy selling brooms and dusters, or perhaps by someone looking for work. This particular Saturday in the late 1990s, the bell announced a visitor who said that the president would like to pay a call.

It did seem rather unlikely. The homeowner looked out

the window to check what was what. Maybe it was some sort of joke, or an opportunistic criminal. And then she heard that famous voice – yes, it was the suburb's high-profile new resident, Nelson Mandela.

The residents of that Houghton street saw quite a bit of their famous neighbour. He often took walks in the road. On his walks, he would stop to chat to gardeners cutting lawns or trimming trees, and to domestic workers walking to work. Occasionally, he paid surprise visits to his neighbours, showing an interest in their lives, and particularly asking after their families. Neighbour Mike Jacklin mentioned that his son was living in London, and Mandela urged him to tell him to come back. And then he phoned the young man himself, calling London from his dad's sitting room in Houghton.

He occasionally invited neighbours into his home. There are precious memories and photographs of kids having tea with Madiba and Graça.

MANDELA
THE
ELDER

LATE BLOOMING LOVE

On his 80th birthday, Nelson Mandela married Graça Machel. Like all of Mandela's life story, the romance was a remarkable tale. She was the widow of Mozambican president Samora Machel, who died in a mysterious plane crash in South Africa in 1986. Twenty-seven years younger than Mandela, she had trained as a soldier in Frelimo, the Mozambican liberation movement, and had been Mozambique's first Minister of Education after independence from Portugal. And he, 27 years in prison, twice married, ex-president – well, he was Nelson Mandela.

They first met when Mandela, newly released from prison, visited Mozambique. Two years later, when they met again in Cape Town, Mandela was separated from Winnie. Their friendship grew and blossomed. Graça was, in many ways, the perfect companion for Mandela. Like him, she had known long years of struggle and suffering and had fought for dignity and justice. And then there was her intellect and integrity, her warm vivacious manner, her commitment to children's issues.

Before long, he was talking openly about being in love. When they travelled together he held her hand. Or gave her a kiss. They took a stroll around the neighbourhood near his house, his arm around her shoulders. The stately Mandela was showing all the signs of infatuation.

'I cannot describe my joy and happiness to receive the love and warmth of such a humble but gracious and brilliant lady,' Mandela wrote at the time. 'It gives me unbelievable comfort and satisfaction to know that there [is] somebody somewhere in the universe on whom I can rely, especially on matters where my political comrades cannot provide me.'

Marriage, though, was out of the question. Machel had her own life and family and responsibilities in Mozambique. And besides, who knew how South Africans, or Mozambicans, would react to such a union of their revered leaders? Delightedly, as it turned out. Who doesn't love a love story, after all? The disintegration of Mandela's marriage to Winnie had been deeply painful, and, despite being one of the world's most beloved figures, he had been lonely. South Africans were, by and large, thrilled to see him so happy. And if any man should be a worthy companion for the Mozambicans' beloved former first lady surely it was Nelson Mandela. The citizens of both countries were pleased by this romantic turn of events.

A small, private wedding was secretly arranged for the day of Mandela's 80th birthday, 18 July 1998. Family and a handful of friends – Ahmed Kathrada and the Sisulus and former warder Christo Brand among them – witnessed the couple's blessing in the Jewish, Muslim and Hindu faiths, and their marriage by the Methodist Bishop Mvume Dandala, aided by the retired Archbishop Desmond Tutu, who had long been gently pressuring the couple to make things official. Astonishingly, there was only one journalist, Jon Qwelane, in attendance.

The 80th birthday party the next day doubled as a massive wedding feast. It couldn't have been more different from the intimate gathering of the previous day. It was a who's who of South African politicos and celebs, family and friends, plus international dignitaries. Nina Simone was there, and Michael Jackson. Thabo Mbeki made a speech, quoting *King Lear*. Mandela's speech spoke of South Africa's children and paid special tribute to those who cared for and fostered them. Eighty children lit the candles on his cake. Stevie Wonder led the 2000 guests in a rousing rendition of 'Happy Birthday', and the man of the moment did his famous Madiba jive.

And when he opened his remarks with 'My wife and I . . .', the room exploded in thunderous applause.

OPRAH'S GIFT

'When you go to Nelson Mandela's house, what do you take?' wondered Oprah Winfrey. 'You can't bring a candle.'

Fair question. What *do* you give as a thank-you gift when you're the house guest of an icon?

Oprah faced this tricky social dilemma when she and her partner, Stedman Graham, spent a ten-day vacation with Mandela in the Western Cape in 2002. Oprah had felt a strong connection to the country since her first trip in 1995, soon after the first democratic elections – and was inspired by Nelson and Winnie Mandela's activism. And now she was to spend a whole holiday with him.

Oprah described her time with Mandela in his home as one of the great honours of her life. She was intimidated at first, she wrote in an article in *Forbes* magazine: 'I'd said to my partner, Stedman, "What am I going to talk about for ten days and ten nights at Nelson Mandela's house?" And Stedman said, "Why don't you try listening?"'

So she did. Gradually, she got comfortable just hanging out with him. One day, over newspapers and tea, they got chatting about what was in the news: poverty and how to change it. Oprah said: 'The only way to change poverty is through education, and one day I would like to build a school in South Africa.' The next thing she knew, Mandela was on his feet, and calling the Minister of Education. By that afternoon she was in a meeting, talking about building a school.

She wrote that she had been thinking about how best to use her charitable efforts in a way that resonated with her spirit. And through Mandela's inspiration she found her answer – a leadership academy for girls from the same poor, dysfunctional and lonely background she herself had emerged from. Coupled with a sense of resilience and hope.

She pledged $10 million towards the construction of the Oprah Winfrey Leadership Academy for Girls at Henley on Klip, south of Johannesburg. The academy opened its doors five years later, in 2007. On 2 January, Nelson Mandela, by then retired, came to open the new school.

So, Oprah Winfrey found the perfect gift for her host. As she hoped, she left behind something that would be of value.

TAKING ACTION ON HIV/AIDS

In 2002, Nelson Mandela paid a visit to a man who – in a different way from Madiba – was prepared to risk his own life for the people of his country. Treatment Action Campaign (TAC) activist Zackie Achmat was HIV-positive. He was able to take expensive, life-saving antiretroviral (ARV) medications because generous friends helped with the cost. Knowing that the majority of South African HIV-positive people could not afford ARVs, and could not access affordable treatment in the public healthcare sector, Achmat refused to use the ARVs. It was a question of equality, he said. Until the government made them available in the public sector, he wouldn't take the medicines. He became gravely ill as a result.

Mandela visited Achmat to try to persuade him to take his treatment, but was unsuccessful. But he agreed with Achmat's request that he take the TAC message to the ANC's national executive committee.

Months later, the former president was visiting an HIV clinic run by the humanitarian organisation Médecins Sans Frontières on the Cape Flats. TAC activists had been wearing T-shirts emblazoned with the words 'HIV POSITIVE' to marches, to symbolise the struggle for openness and justice around HIV. Mandela put on an 'HIV POSITIVE' T-shirt. It was an extraordinary moment, a bold gesture at a time when Mandela's successor, Thabo Mbeki, and his government were questioning the science around the link between HIV and Aids, and dragging their heels on rolling out treatment.

Once he saw that, Achmat said he knew he could take his pills. He didn't have to die. Mandela's support turned the tide.

Mandela had been criticised for the government's lack of leadership and lack of action on HIV/Aids during his presidency. Admittedly, the new government had its hands full building the young democracy, but, nonetheless, a proactive approach might have helped stem the steady rise in new HIV infections during that time. A forceful approach from Mandela himself, with his unrivalled moral authority, could have made a real difference.

In January 2005, Mandela dealt a blow to the stigmatisation and silence around HIV when he announced that his 54-year-old son, Makgatho, had died of Aids. 'Let us give publicity to HIV/Aids and not hide it, because the only way to make it appear like a normal illness, like TB, like cancer, is always to come out and to say somebody has died because of HIV,' Mandela said at Makgatho's funeral. 'And people will stop regarding it as something extraordinary.'

Later in life, Madiba became an ardent campaigner. In fact, he devoted most of his public time and attention to HIV/Aids. His charity – called 46664 after his prison number – raised both funds and awareness.

ETERNAL FLAME OF DEMOCRACY

On 10 December 2011, at his home in Qunu, the 93-year-old Nelson Mandela lit the Flame of Democracy that was to burn at Constitution Hill. The flame was taken from the candle lit by Mandela, and then transported across the country for about a thousand kilometres, from the rolling hills of the remote Eastern Cape to the busy metropolis of Johannesburg.

11 December 2011 marked the 15th anniversary of the signing of the Constitution. The flame that Mandela had lit was used by then Deputy President Kgalema Motlanthe to ignite the Flame of Democracy. The flame passed through

the hands of each of the Constitutional Court judges before touching the bowl. Motlanthe said: 'We must light the flame to dispel the darkness of our past. The Eternal Flame of Democracy that we are lighting today must never blow out but for ever cast light on our nation.'

The Flame of Democracy burns outside the Court in one of the four remaining stand-alone staircases of what was once the awaiting-trial block of the Old Fort Prison precinct. Mandela was held in this very block, as one of 156 activists arrested and charged in the historic Treason Trial. The perpetual flame signifies the country's commitment to democracy, human rights and constitutionalism.

THE MANDELA MOVIE

When producer Anant Singh first considered making a film based on the life of Nelson Mandela, he couldn't have envisaged that it would take nearly two decades to come to the screen, or that its release would coincide so poignantly with the great man's death.

Being politically active and in the film business, Singh had long been drawn to the idea of making a film about Mandela. He first made contact through Fatima Meer, author of the 1988 authorised biography, *Higher Than Hope*. Mandela was still in prison, and the two men began to correspond about the possibility. Mandela wasn't totally convinced of the idea of a film about his life. In fact, he wondered modestly whether anyone would be interested in seeing it.

Singh describes his meeting with Mandela, just two weeks after his release from prison, as a wonderful experience: 'You come into the room just in awe of him and he makes you feel comfortable. We talked about many things, from global politics to family. He was so caring and so interested in my point of view. He told me about *Long Walk to Freedom*, his autobiography, which had been smuggled out of prison, and we decided to wait until that was published to make the movie.'

Plenty of filmmakers, including major studios, vied for the rights to the book, but Mandela liked the idea of a South African making the movie. Knowing Singh, and his history as a filmmaker, Mandela awarded him the rights. It was a great honour and a great responsibility for Singh.

'Mandela said: "I trust you, I want you to make this movie, don't bother me." What he did say, which I thought said a lot about him, was: "Show me for my weaknesses before my strengths."

'He was such a remarkable human being, even with the failures in his relationships, and his family life. He had these amazing qualities – humility and leadership and integrity. It made him the perfect character to portray in the film. That was the easy part. The difficult part was doing it in two hours. I could have made a ten-hour miniseries, but

I wanted to make a feature film. It was a daunting task, which is why it took so long to get made. There were 70 different drafts, eight writers, several directors. Once we homed in on the love story, that made it work.'

Mandela didn't get to see the completed film, but he did see some of the footage. Singh travelled to Qunu to show it to him: 'I spent the day with him. He was impressed with what he saw. He remembered the characters, and talked about them. It was great for me, given the journey that we had been on with the film, and the relationship he and my family had built up over the years.'

Long Walk to Freedom premiered in London on 5 December 2013, as a Royal Film Performance. Singh describes the scene: 'It was a fancy red-carpet event in London. Zindzi and Zenani were with us that evening as our guests. Kate and William were there with their entourage. It was a really special, joyous evening.'

The film had already started when Zindzi and Zenani got the news of Mandela's death and went back to their hotel. 'I asked if we should stop the film. They said, no, Madiba wouldn't want that, so we carried on,' says Singh.

As the credits rolled, Anant Singh took to the stage, with actor Idris Elba beside him, to break the news. 'When we came out, the audience thought we were up there for accolades, but when they heard, people were in shock. They were weeping. It was a surreal experience.' Prince William briefly addressed the press as he left the theatre.

Singh remembers Mandela with great fondness and respect: 'Over the years we became friends we saw this unique quality, how he was with all people, from all walks of life, from kings to the bellman in the hotel, or the people working in the kitchen.'

MANDELA'S DREAM – A HOSPITAL FOR THE CHILDREN

You can forget what you know about hospitals when you walk into the Nelson Mandela Children's Hospital (NMCH) in Johannesburg. There is no medical smell, no grey corridors, no long lines and no air of fear and foreboding. Instead, imagine an airy, colourful, comfortable space where children – and their families – can feel at peace and at home. The technology and equipment is among the most advanced in the world.

If you know anything about Nelson Mandela, you know that he took great joy in children, and cared deeply about their welfare. He wanted to create a state-of-the-art, child-centred paediatric hospital to serve the children of South Africa and the region. The NMCH is the fulfilment of a long-held dream of Mandela's.

In 2005, plans were announced for the Nelson Mandela Children's Hospital, which was to be a flagship project of the Nelson Mandela Children's Fund. It was a huge and ambitious project, not least in terms of funding – it was going to cost R1 billion.

In July 2009, as part of his birthday celebrations, Mandela undertook the site dedication and planted a tree. It was the last official event he did for the hospital. Bongi Mkhabela, CEO of the Nelson Mandela Children's Fund, recalls: 'He was becoming increasingly frail, and we didn't know how much longer we would have him. Our fear was that he wouldn't see this project come to fruition. It was important for him to see a little bit of the future, almost like Moses saying, "I can see the promised land." It was exciting that we broke ground but sad in that we didn't know how long he would be around. His dedicating the site gave us all a huge energy boost. We were in the difficult planning and fundraising phase, but after that there was no going back, we had to do this.'

The Children's Hospital remained a project close to his heart, she says. 'Even when his mind was not very clear, it was very clear on the hospital. Whenever I would see him he would ask, "How's the hospital going?" After he had retired to Qunu, I was there meeting with Mrs Machel, to discuss the hospital. He came in and asked what we were doing, and we said we were having a planning meeting about the hospital, and he said: "Planning? Why are you still planning?"'

The planning finally paid off. The hospital opened its

doors in December 2016. The first patients were admitted in June 2017. Nelson Mandela did not live to see the opening of the hospital that bears his name, but his widow, Graça Machel, herself a staunch advocate of children's rights, is the chair of the hospital's trust.

SING IT RIGHT

Bongi Mkhabela tells a story that illustrates what a stickler Mandela was for doing things correctly, for getting the details right.

'We were in Limpopo for a Children's Fund event around his birthday. The event was being televised. So we start with the national anthem, but we don't sing all of it, because we have limited time on air and we want to have a little bit of the anthem, and a bit of him speaking. So just because of timing, we shorten it, and that means we leave out "Die Stem".

'When we finish, Mandela stands up and says, "No, this is not the national anthem. You will sing it again and you'll sing *all* of it."

'Which we did, of course. We started again and we sang it all. It drove us a bit insane, but you must understand that for him it was around the issue of reconciliation. If you didn't sing all of the national anthem, you compromised an agenda that he believed in very much. No public event was just an event, it was an opportunity to engage people, to influence, to inform, to create the rainbow nation that we talk about.'

CHRISTMAS AT QUNU

Anyone who worked with Mandela in the public realm knew that you were only minutes away from being mobbed. When Mandela went home to Qunu for Christmas, it became a tradition to lay on a Christmas celebration for the kids in the area. It started rather informally, with a couple of hundred children, and the presidential staff, including the bodyguards, roped in to help pack gift parcels. By 2002, when Oprah Winfrey co-hosted the Christmas party with Nelson Mandela, 15 000 children arrived to see Mandela, and to get a gift and a meal.

Having averted a dangerous stampede, Mandela decided to let the Children's Fund, with their extensive experience of organising children's events, take over the organisation of the Christmas party.

Bongi Mkhabela recalls that they had previously planned for 10 000 and got 15 000, so this time they reckoned they might have 20 000, but they would provide for 25 000, just to be on the safe side. A big sponsor was secured, and each child would get a school bag with stationery, a toy, underwear and school clothes.

Mkhabela was there, with her family as volunteers: 'Early in the morning, a colleague called me outside. I stood on the koppie and looked out into the distance, and remarked on what I thought was a forest. My colleague said, 'Look again. Those aren't trees, those are people.' I think 70 000 people came. It totally overwhelmed our systems, and was a complete safety hazard.

'You must understand that when we do Children's Fund events, we are sticklers for caring for the children. We have names, and forms. There is one caregiver per 20 children. There is medical care available and enough water. And now I'm in the middle of crazy! This was terrifying.

'We were giving the gifts away from these huge trucks, but we had to close the trucks and send them away from Qunu, to avoid a stampede. Once the trucks were gone, people started to disperse. And then Mandela and Mrs Machel came out, him wearing his Children's Fund T-shirt, and people started coming back! As a manager, it's a complete nightmare, because he just draws people. He wants to be there, he wants to greet them, he gets energy from their energy.

'At the end of that day when there was no child around, and they were all safe – I'd never had such a sense of relief.

'After that we said, "Tata, we love you and we love the children, but we can't do this again. I wish we could still do it, but we can't."'

WINNING THE WORLD CUP BID

South Africa was one of five countries bidding to host the 2010 Fifa World Cup. Fifa had reserved the tournament for an African country that year, and South Africa was up against Egypt, Morocco, Tunisia and Libya. Having success-fully hosted major international sporting events, such as the 1995 Rugby World Cup and the 2003 Cricket World Cup, counted in the country's favour, but then again, South Africa had been tipped to win – but narrowly lost – the right to stage the 2006 Fifa World Cup.

For the 2010 bid, the bid organisers weren't taking any chances. Nelson Mandela was pressed into service to help South Africa win. He and Archbishop Desmond Tutu flew to the Caribbean to lobby the leaders of the Confederation of North, Central America and Caribbean Association Foot-ball (Concacaf) to support the South African bid.

Mandela, who was 85 when he made the trip in April 2004, told the huge crowd that turned up to see him that he had defied his doctor's orders to come to Trinidad and Tobago. He looked frail and old and in fact said: 'This is my last trip abroad – I am here to plead.'

He might have been frail, but Mandela made an emo-tive case for South Africa's bid, right down to the wire. At a farewell dinner for the bid committee Mandela said: 'We indeed have much to celebrate after a decade of living peacefully together in our thriving democracy. There could be few better gifts for us in this year of our celebration than to be awarded the 2010 Soccer World Cup.'

Days later, he headed for Zürich, to join the South African delegation, which included President Thabo Mbeki, Archbishop Desmond Tutu, former president FW de Klerk and football legend Lucas Radebe. Mandela described how sport had provided release and entertainment on Robben Island, where he was imprisoned, and the role football played in breaking down racial barriers. Archbishop Tutu apparently jokingly promised Fifa executive committee members 'a free ticket to heaven' if they voted for South Africa – 'But don't use it immediately,' he said. It would be safe to say that South Africa pulled out all the stops.

The announcement was made on 15 May 2004. Mandela was sitting in the front of the auditorium when Fifa president Sepp Blatter slowly drew the card from the envelope and announced: 'The 2010 World Cup will be organised by . . . South Africa . . . We can all applaud Africa. The victor is football. The victor is Africa.'

The South African delegation erupted in delight. Mandela smiled as he lifted the World Cup trophy, saying, 'I feel like a young man of 50.' Back home, the joyful blasting of vuvuzelas could be heard countrywide, as South Africans celebrated and partied as if they'd already won.

DON'T CALL ME, I'LL CALL YOU . . .

Shortly before his 86th birthday, in 2004, Mandela called a press conference. His diary and public activities were to be significantly reduced and his time spent on family, friends and himself, he said. 'One of the things that made me long to be back in prison was that I had so little opportunity for reading, thinking and quiet reflection after my release. I intend, amongst other things, to give myself much more opportunity for such reading and reflection.'

He went on to make an appeal: 'Henceforth I want to be in the position of calling you to ask whether I would be welcome, rather than being called upon to do things and participate in events. The appeal therefore is: don't call me, I'll call you . . . We trust that people will understand our considerations and will grant us the opportunity for a much quieter life. And I thank all of you in anticipation for your consideration.'

He ended with his trademark charm and self-deprecating humour: 'Thank you very much for your attention and thank you for being kind to an old man – allowing him to take a rest, even if many of you may feel that after loafing somewhere on an island and other places for 27 years the rest is not really deserved.'

But Mandela did not get the quieter life he desired. Verne Harris, Director of Archive and Dialogue at the Nelson Mandela Foundation, who worked with Mandela from 2004, said: 'He was subject to endless demands. And as he got older, it was worse, he was used and manipulated.'

Not everyone was sensitive to his wish for peace, or to his diminishing health. His hearing aids made it difficult for him to hear and to focus with a lot of noise about, and from about 2006 it was communicated that he did not like to be with more than three people at a time. And yet people continued to arrive in big groups.

He used to call the people on his staff 'my warders', says Harris. 'It was a joke, but he was also saying that he was not really free.' He sometimes found a way to put his foot down, though. Harris tells a story from his own experience in 2010:

'Kathy Kathrada and I were working on a project together. We had a number of questions which only Madiba could answer. We went over to his house and found him relaxing and just about to start reading the newspapers.

'I could see he was irritated at the prospect of a work-related discussion. After our introductory remarks and detailing of the questions, he responded: "Chaps, at my age one remembers some things and not others. Now, I don't remember any of the things you're asking me about. Do you mind if I read my papers?"

'We had been dismissed. That was the last time I went to Madiba with a work matter.'

DARE NOT LINGER

Long Walk to Freedom, Nelson Mandela's wonderful auto-biography, ends with his inauguration as president of South Africa, and with these words: 'I have taken a moment here to rest, to steal a view of the glorious vista that surrounds me, to look back on the distance I have come. But I can rest only for a moment, for with freedom comes responsibilities, and I dare not linger, for my long walk is not yet ended.'

Towards the end of his presidency, Mandela started work on a second book, covering his years as president of South Africa. He never completed it. When he died, he left behind around 70 000 words. Celebrated novelist Mandla Langa was given the task of shaping Nelson Mandela's handwritten draft into a coherent and compelling book. Echoing that last line of *Long Walk to Freedom*, he called the book *Dare Not Linger*.

After a brief moment of 'This is crazy, I'm not going to do this!', Langa set to work: 'It was daunting at first. As a novelist I've been in control of the characters. Here was the world's most recognised icon and I had to make sure that his voice carried through. There was a sense of respect, but I knew I had to do what I had to do. We pay homage to a person when we are as free as possible when depicting or interpreting a figure, rather than when we defer to them all the time. I tried to accept him and see him in all his complexity.'

Langa spent a year writing and researching. Fortunately, Mandela was a meticulous note-taker, and, along with the original drafts, Langa had access to Mandela's detailed notes made as events unfolded. And then there was the personal input from Mandela's widow, Graça Machel, his speech-writers Joel Netshitenzhe and Tony Trew, and others. The result is an illuminating memoir that gives insight into the events of those remarkable years and Mandela's own thoughts about them, and the context in which they took place.

With this mammoth project behind him, Langa has, per-haps, a unique insight into Mandela, his legacy and how he is seen today: 'On the one hand, we have this teddy-bear kind of version of the man. The reconciliation junky. We forget that this was the man who was volunteer-in-chief of the Defiance Campaign. To put that into perspective, it was four years since the Nationalist Party had come to power. South Africa was a very rough place to be black and involved in the oppositional politics, and he said, "I will be the face of this, I will be the leader . . ." We have not al-ways appreciated the guts that takes.

'Then when he started the negotiations, that was a very difficult thing to do. In a sense, he forced the hand of the ANC. There was incredible resistance within the ANC. But he pushed. The ANC found itself caught up in a momentum where they almost had to follow him. And I look at how he handled the right wing at the time of negotiation. That was a very tricky situation. Anything could have happened.'

Revisionists have started to question aspects of Mandela's legacy: was he too focused on reconciliation, too appeasing of the white minority?

It's inevitable, said Langa, that, as with any historical figure, there are a lot of questions. People look at him through the lens of today, sometimes losing sight of the particular dynamics and pressures of the time, the kind of forces that were ranged against him and his mission towards this democratic South Africa.

'Nelson Mandela was preoccupied with stability, with creating conditions for democracy. He believed the next step would take place when he passes the baton to others, that they are going to deal with some of the issues.

'There should have been, I think, a lot more attention paid to the question of the economy, issues of land redistribution, during the negotiations. The economic degradation goes back centuries. We are still living with the effects of that. What we have not done is build on his legacy to create a much more liveable democracy.

'But hindsight is an exact science. And there is the disappointment with the current set of circumstances, and that accrues as criticism against Nelson Mandela – "if only he had done this or that". It is understandable, but sometimes disappointing.

'What would South Africa have been like without Mandela? I think it would have been a wasteland. We would have been at each other's throats. We would not have a functioning democracy, that's for sure. Mandela helped us to know what it means to be a South African, to walk in the world with our heads held high.'

HAMBA KAHLE TATA

Late on Thursday 5 December 2013, South Africans heard the news – Nelson Mandela was dead. He had passed away at the age of 95, from a prolonged respiratory infection.

The nation had been expecting and dreading the news for weeks, but despite this, and despite his age, when it happened they were bereft.

They did what human beings do in grief: they gathered together to mourn and remember, to weep and to give thanks. Through the night and the Friday morning, and on through the week, people arrived outside his house in Houghton. They brought flowers and notes and photographs and candles, and made impromptu pavement shrines. They brought children and babies and took photographs and selfies. They cried and sang and prayed. On the grassy sidewalk, children spelled out with rocks: 'We love you Mandela.'

In Vilikazi Street in Soweto, people gathered, some draped

in ANC colours, and sang the songs they sang in the struggle years to protest his incarceration, the lyrics now imbued with new meaning: 'We have not seen Mandela in the place where he is, in the place where he is kept.'

For ten days, the nation mourned. Throughout the country, in places of worship, in public squares, in schools and offices, they paid tribute. Memorial services were held. Flags flew at half-mast not only in Madiba's homeland but also at US government buildings and at Buckingham Palace. Vigils were held and moments of silence observed the world over. At the Grammy nominations in Los Angeles and the drawing ceremony for the 2014 Fifa World Cup in Brazil and the South African embassy in Tehran.

They felt South Africa's loss as their own.

The official memorial service was held at Johannesburg's FNB Stadium on 10 December, on an unusually chilly and rainy day. Kings and presidents and pop stars came to pay their respects. Over 70 heads of state. Four American presidents. Oprah and Bono. Kenneth Kaunda. Kofi Annan.

More than 100 000 people viewed his body as it lay in state at the Union Buildings in Pretoria. In the same place that they watched his inauguration as their first democratically elected president, they came to bid him farewell.

A state funeral was held on 15 December 2013 at Qunu, in the Eastern Cape. With the love and thanks of the nation he liberated, Nelson Mandela was laid to rest in the gentle rolling hills he had roamed as a child, dreamed of in prison, and longed for in his retirement.

SOURCES

1 Mandela the boy

Of donkeys and dishonour: Nelson Mandela, *Long Walk to Freedom*, Macdonald Purnell, 1994, p 10.

Becoming a man: Mandela, *Long Walk to Freedom*, p 24.

Broadening horizons: Mandela, *Long Walk to Freedom*, p 39.

Among the intellectual elite: Mandela, *Long Walk to Freedom*, p 45.

Principals and principles: Mandela, *Long Walk to Freedom*, p 49.

Escape to the city of gold: '"I Will Go Singing": Walter Sisulu Speaks of His Life and Struggle for Freedom', interview with George M Houser and Herbert Shore, 1995. South African History Online. Available at www.sahistory.org.za, accessed on 20 February 2018.

2 Mandela the young man

Founding the ANC Youth League: Mandela, *Long Walk to Freedom*, p 94.

First love: Mandela, *Long Walk to Freedom*, p 193.

'When I met Mandela . . .': George Bizos, *65 Years of Friendship*, Umuzi, 2015, p 25.

Defiance Campaign volunteer-in-chief: Mandela, *Long Walk to Freedom*, p 122.

Mandela and Tambo Attorneys: Glenn Frankel, *Rivonia's Children*, Jacana, 2011, p 49; Dikgang Moseneke, *My Own Liberator: A Memoir*, Picador Africa, 2016, p 207; Luli Callinicos, *The World that Made Mandela*, Real African Publishers, 2000.

In the ring and on the road: Mandela, *Long Walk to Freedom*, p 180.

The policeman's knock on the door . . .: Rusty Bernstein, *Memory Against Forgetting: Memoirs from a Life in South African Politics*,

Viking, 1999; Helen Joseph, *If This Be Treason*, André Deutsch, 1963.

3 Mandela on the run

The Black Pimpernel: Ahmed Kathrada, *Memoirs*, Zebra Press, 2005, p 148.

The Spear of the Nation: Mandela, *Long Walk to Freedom*, p 262.

Seeking Africa's support for the struggle: Mandela, *Long Walk to Freedom*, p 283.

Travelling boots: Penny Dale, 'The man who taught Mandela to be a soldier', BBC News, 9 December 2013.

Courtroom drama – and jail time: Mandela, *Long Walk to Freedom*, p 311.

4 Mandela the prisoner

The State vs Nelson Mandela and Others: Anthony Sampson, *Mandela: The Authorised Biography*, HarperCollins, 1999, p 196; 'Statement by Albert Luthuli on the conclusion of the Rivonia Trial', 12 June 1964. Available at www.anc.org.za, accessed on 6 March 2018.

The joker: Christo Brand, *Doing Life with Mandela*, Jonathan Ball, 2014, p 77.

Taking the struggle to the island: Sampson, *Mandela*, p 206; *Long Walk to Freedom*, p 376; interview with Fikile Bam, *PBS Frontline*, no date. Available at www.pbs.org, accessed on 6 March 2018; Mandela, *Long Walk to Freedom*, p 404; Neville Alexander, *Robben Island Prison Dossier*, UCT Press, 1994, p 34.

Holding the baby: Brand, *Doing Life with Mandela*, p 33.

Know your enemy . . .: interview with Fikile Bam, *PBS Frontline*, no date.

Cold comfort and icy showers: Kathrada, *Memoirs*, p 203.

Letters from inside: Ghaleb Cachalia, interview with the author, January 2018.

Heartbreaking news from home: Mandela, *Long Walk to Freedom*, p 99; Nelson Mandela Centre of Memory, 'Mandela gets closure on 1969 death of eldest son', *TimesLive*, 22 February 2012. Available at www.timeslive.co.za, accessed on 6 March 2018.

'Here you are amongst friends': 'Ronnie Mamoepa remembers his time and Madiba in jail', SABC Digital News, 13 December 2013. Available at www.youtube.com/watch?v=PCAztaMkQKE, accessed on 6 March 2018. Lionel Davis, interview with the author, January 2018.

5 Mandela the negotiator

The power of touch: Mandela, *Long Walk to Freedom*, p 505.

Last stop on the road to freedom: Mandela, *Long Walk to Freedom*, p 537.

Freedom for some: Mandela, *Long Walk to Freedom*, p 547.

6 Mandela walks free

Making friends and winning support: John Carlin, *Knowing Mandela: A Personal Portrait*, Atlantic Books, 2013; Robin Renwick, *Mission to South Africa: Diary of a Revolution*, Jonathan Ball, 2015, p 137.

Mandela and Tambo, together again: Valli Moosa, interview with the author, January 2018.

Free Mandela (from Mrs Thatcher!): Renwick, *Mission to South Africa*, pp 142–143.

In the ring with Ali: BBC News, 'Muhammad Ali letter to Nelson Mandela sold for £7,200', 17 December 2016.

Don't mess with Mandela: Danny Schechter, *Madiba A to Z: The Many Faces of Nelson Mandela*, Jacana, 2013, p 24.

A surprise visit from the President: Debora Patta, interview with the author, January 2018.

The native who caused all the trouble: John Kani, interview with the author, January 2018.

Charming the journos: Rich Mkhondo, interview with the author, January 2018.

Conflict about the Nobel Peace Prize: Bizos, *65 Years of Friendship*, p 214; Sampson, *Mandela*, p 474.

7 Mandela as president

Mandela casts his vote: Mandela, *Long Walk to Freedom*, p 610.

A new South Africa, a new president: Bill Keller, 'Mandela is named president, closing the era of apartheid', *The New York Times*, 9 May 1994.

There is no more you and us: Rory Steyn, interview with the author, January 2018.

It's all about the children: Bongi Mkhabela, interview with the author, January 2018.

Cooking fit for a king: Brett Ladds, interview with the author, January 2018.

It was the time of my life . . .: Vanessa Mitchell, interview with the author, January 2018.

Melktert in Orania: Amina Cachalia, *When Hope and History Rhyme: An Autobiography*, Picador Africa, 2013, p 2.

Dancing with the Queen: Renwick, *Mission to South Africa*, p 174.

Reach for a Dream: Kathrada, *Memoirs*, p 361.

'Asimbonanga' – We have not seen him . . .: Johnny Clegg, interview with the author, January 2018; 'Johnny Clegg (with Nelson Mandela) – Asimbonanga 1999 [1997]', YouTube, published 17 August 2007. Available at www.youtube.com/watch?v=BGS7SpI7obY, accessed on 6 March 2018.

Two presidents: Rich Mkhondo, 'Laughing his way through life', *The Star*, 9 December 2013. Available at www.iol.co.za, accessed on 6 March 2018; Scott Pelley, 'Bill Clinton talks about his friendship with Nelson Mandela', CBS News, 5 December 2013.

Hello, neighbour: eNCA, 'Madiba's neighbours reflect on their friend',

7 December 2013. Available at www.enca.com, accessed on 27 February 2018.

8 Mandela the elder

Late blooming love: Nelson Mandela, *Conversations With Myself,* Pan Macmillan, 2010.

The Mandela movie: Anant Singh, interview with the author, January 2018.

Mandela's dream – a hospital for the children: Bongi Mkhabela, interview with the author, January 2018.

Sing it right: Bongi Mkhabela, interview with the author, January 2018.

Christmas at Qunu: Bongi Mkhabela, interview with the author, January 2018.

Winning the World Cup bid: Staff Reporter, 'How Madiba was strong-armed in World Cup bid', *Mail & Guardian*, 12 May 2006. Available at mg.co.za, accessed on 6 March 2018.

Don't call me, I'll call you . . .: Verne Harris, interview with the author, January 2018.

Dare Not Linger: Mandela, *Long Walk to Freedom*, p 617; Mandla Langa, interview with the author, January 2018.

Selected bibliography

Alexander, Neville, *Robben Island Prison Dossier*, UCT Press, 1994.

Bernstein, Rusty, *Memory Against Forgetting: Memoirs from a Life in South African Politics*, Viking, 1999.

Bizos, George, *65 Years of Friendship*, Umuzi, 2015.

Brand, Christo, *Doing Life with Mandela*, Jonathan Ball, 2014.

Cachalia, Amina, *When Hope and History Rhyme: An Autobiography*, Picador Africa, 2013.

Callinicos, Luli, *The World that Made Mandela*, Real African Publishers, 2000.

Carlin, John, *Knowing Mandela: A Personal Portrait*, Atlantic Books, 2013.

Du Preez Bezdrob, Anné Mariè, *Winnie Mandela: A Life*, Zebra Press, 2003.

Frankel, Glenn, *Rivonia's Children*, Jacana, 2011.

Joseph, Helen, *If This Be Treason*, André Deutsch, 1963.

Kathrada, Ahmed, *Memoirs*, Zebra Press, 2004.

Mandela, Nelson, *Long Walk to Freedom*, Macdonald Purnell, 1994.

Mandela, Nelson, *Conversations With Myself*, Pan Macmillan, 2010.

Mandela, Nelson and Mandla Langa, *Dare Not Linger: The Presidential Years*, Pan Macmillan, 2017.

Moseneke, Dikgang, *My Own Liberator: A Memoir*, Picador Africa, 2016.

Renwick, Robin, *Mission to South Africa: Diary of a Revolution*, Jonathan Ball, 2015.

Sampson, Anthony, *Mandela: The Authorised Biography*, Harper-Collins, 1999.

Schechter, Danny, *Madiba A to Z: The Many Faces of Nelson Mandela*, Jacana, 2013.

KATE SIDLEY is a writer, editor, reviewer and columnist who works for a wide range of magazines and newspapers, in print and online, as well as on radio. She is the author of the book *The Agony Chef*, and co-writer of the play *Shape*.